ENDORSEME

You read a good book becomes an ... strengthens your call and clarifies your focus. Greg has written a remarkable little book. Pastors, elders, youth leaders, parents and students should bless themselves by reading Firing Jesus.

—Derwin L. Gray, Lead Pastor,
Transformation Church, Charlotte, NC

Firing Jesus highlights exactly why Jesus is described in the Bible as a "stumbling stone" and a "rock of offense"—He's nothing like the attentive butler and nice-guy genie He's often been reduced into in a culture that's in love with spirituality but at war with the "exclusivity" of Jesus. Greg Stier is passionate about Jesus and the person-to-person spread of His gospel, and *Firing Jesus* vividly re-imagines how that "rock of offense" would turn the tables on the complacent power structures inherent in many of today's churches. If you're a youth worker, this is a must-read.

—Rick Lawrence, Executive Editor, GROUP Magazine
Author of *Jesus-Centered Youth Ministry*

Greg Stier is a prolific soul winner who without a compromise speaks truth to the hearts of saved and unsaved. This book forces you to look inside yourself, but please don't just look if you feel the voice of God speaking to you to change. PLEASE change!

—Reggie Dabbs, Motivational Youth Speaker

Firing Jesus has the capacity to radically change the way everyone looks at teenagers. I pray that more youth leaders will encourage evangelism as a lifestyle, not a thing-you-do-once-a-year-on-a-mission-trip-or-after-a-youth-conference. This book is a vehicle to drive people to that kind of passionate faith.

—Katie Payne, Student

FIRING JESUS

GREG STIER

Firing Jesus

Copyright © 2012 by Dare 2 Share Ministries, Inc.
All rights reserved.

A D2S Publishing book

All scripture quotations, unless otherwise indicated, are taken from the Holy Bible, New International Version®, NIV®. Copyright ©1973, 1978, 1984, 2011 by Biblica, Inc.™ Used by permission of Zondervan. All rights reserved worldwide. www.zondervan.com The "NIV" and "New International Version" are trademarks registered in the United States Patent and Trademark Office by Biblica, Inc.™

This is a work of fiction. With the exception of known historical characters, all characters are the product of the author's imagination.

No part of this publication may be reproduced, stored in a retrieval system, or transmitted in any form or by any means—electronic, mechanical, photocopy, recording, or otherwise—without prior permission of the publisher.

Editor: Jane Dratz

Stier, Greg.
Firing Jesus / by Greg Stier.

ISBN: 978-0-9857352-0-3

Library of Congress Control Number: 2012941454

Printed in the United States of America

1 2 3 4 5 6 7 8 9 / 12 11 10 09 08 07 06

To all the youth leaders who put
their jobs on the line every day
by acting like Jesus.

1

THE EMERGENCY MEETING

"Sorry this meeting was so last minute, guys," Pastor Ryan Coleman apologized as he fumbled with his keys on the front doorstep of Spring Valley Community Church. Three other members of the elder board clustered around him on the chilly March evening. The church secretary, a petite, spry older lady, hurried up the walk to join them, emerging silently from the now ominously dark parking lot.

"No problem," assured Scott West. "Your message sounded urgent and we don't get too many emergency elder meetings around here."

"It is urgent," Pastor Ryan affirmed. "It's very urgent."

"It better be," joked Pete Fisher. "I had to leave the fire station even though it was on fire."

All of them laughed, though even a casual observer could see that Ryan's and Scott's efforts to join in the humor were clearly forced. Together they made their way into the church's office area where Pastor Ryan guided them into the smallest conference room.

"I thought you were working tonight, Pete," commented Ryan.

"Yeah, there was a mix up. But I'm glad of it, because I wouldn't want to miss this meeting. Saw it on my iPhone," Pete responded, holding it up in his large, calloused hands with a smile. "So what's the big emergency?"

"I'll tell everyone in just a few minutes. Let's all get situated, make sure everyone who is gonna show up, shows up, and then I'll explain what's happening."

Pete had the distinct feeling that Ryan didn't expect—or want—him to be there. This made him all the more eager to find out what was going on.

As they sat waiting for others to arrive, Sam Brooke wondered to himself why they were meeting in the small conference room with only five metal chairs drawn around the small, circular table. After all, there were currently a total of seven elders on the church's board, counting the senior pastor and executive pastor. Then with the non-voting church secretary who took the minutes added into the mix, meetings typically topped out at eight. But before he asked the question, Sam thought to himself that there was probably some legitimate reason they couldn't meet in their usual room. After all, more chairs could be squeezed in around the little table. He remained silent.

That was Sam. He liked to give people the benefit of the doubt. He had only been an elder at the church for two years and had a reputation for being traditional, wise and, well, quiet. He didn't speak much, but when he did, he spoke with a sense of authority. Not from a loud voice, but from a life that screamed a steady, stalwart consistency. He had lost his wife to cancer three years earlier and had weathered that storm with grace. He was a kind soul who moved with a gentle strength around the church. Kids would flock to him on Sunday morning for their free piece of candy—if they quoted a Bible verse, of course. Though quiet, no elder meeting was ever complete without Sam's unassuming wisdom and practical insights stirred into the mix.

On the other side of the decibel scale was Scott West. He was loud and proud—proud of his charter member status in the church, proud of his successful church construction business, proud of his position as chairman of the elder board, proud of his ability to make things happen. Although he and the senior pastor often clashed, he usually got the best of it. He knew the church constitution better than the Bible, and he knew the Bible better than most. It was his influence that got Ryan Coleman hired in the first place.

Ryan had not been the elder board's first choice as the executive pastor. Most of the guys still thought he was too young—if 30 is young—and needed some more ministry experience. Sure, he had been a youth pastor for four years out of seminary, but that seemed hardly enough experience to be the EP of a church of 500. But Scott saw in him what he called "a hunger to learn," which would be important when Ryan took the reins of leadership once Senior Pastor Jonathon Griffith eventually moved on—which Scott intended to make certain was only a matter of time. In reality, Ryan's "hunger to learn" was really just a moldable nature that Scott "the potter" took advantage of to implement his own agenda at the church.

Scott was not an alpha dog nearly as much as he was an alpha wolf. When he howled the dogs heeled, the cats hid and most of the other elders peed a little in their pants.

One of the few elders who didn't make lemonade was Pete Fisher. He was equal parts funny and fearless. In his late thirties, he had been a volunteer in the youth ministry for the last five years. He was what some would call an "advocate" for youth ministry on the elder board. A few months back when it was time to find a new youth leader, he'd strongly advocated hiring the current youth guy, JC Davidson. Pete was the one who regularly brought prayer requests from the youth ministry to the bi-weekly elders meeting. If the youth group had to sell burritos to raise money for their annual mission trip to Haiti, Pete brought the salsa, forks and cash. He'd end up buying ten, himself—every time. As a firefighter he was busy when he was busy and free when he was free. He used his free time to mentor teenagers in the group. His shift had got cut short that day because of a scheduling mix up so he, much to Ryan's surprise, was able to make the emergency meeting.

Completing the not-so-complete gathering was Agnes, the sometimes crotchety but always faithful church secretary—she refused the title "executive assistant." She had been on staff long enough to see the rise and fall of the Fax machine. Nobody really knew her age, but she had to be pushing seventy-five. She had, as she loved to remind everyone, lived through the tenure of four pastors at Spring Valley Community Church, including the founding pastor.

Scott pulled Ryan out into the hall and was talking quietly and intensely about something as Agnes and Pete chatted, while Sam listened and smiled.

Finally, Scott and Ryan came back into the room, settling noisily into their chairs as Ryan declared, “Well, let’s get this meeting started.”

Agnes interrupted, “Well, Pastor Griffith isn’t here yet.”

“Agnes,” Scott said drily, “thanks for reminding us of the obvious, but Article 3, Section 24 of the church bylaws states that emergency meetings can be held with or without the pastor, as long as he’s received the same notification about it as the rest of the elder board.” Turning to Ryan he asked, “Didn’t you send that same email you sent to the entire elder board to Pastor Griffith, as well?”

“I sure did,” Ryan affirmed.

Sam uncharacteristically piped in, “That email was sent two hours ago. What did he say when you called him?”

“Um...,” Ryan stumbled, “I couldn’t get a hold of him.” This surprised nobody. Pastor Griffith had a habit of turning his phone off on Sunday afternoons for his post-sermon nap.

“You got a call *and* an email?” asked Pete. “I just got an email and would have missed that if I didn’t have my new iPhone,” He raised it again, but this time not jokingly.

Ryan suddenly turned red with embarrassment. “Sorry, Pete, I must have forgotten to call you.”

Pete was silent, a something’s-not-right feeling rising up in his spaghetti-filled gut.

Elder Jim Simpson’s bulky frame suddenly filled the doorway of the small meeting room.

"Let me grab one more chair," Ryan said, jumping up quickly, grateful for the distraction from the awkwardness surrounding Pete's question.

Fifty-six year old Jim Simpson, an account manager for a large insurance company, was a dependable member of the Scott/Ryan voting block on the church board. Jim rarely deviated from Scott's and Ryan's viewpoint on all matters church related. His arrival reassured Ryan that things were still well under control, despite the unanticipated appearance of Pete Fisher at the quickly called meeting.

"Well, regardless of the pastor's naptime and disregard of an emergency email, we have a quorum, so this meeting must go on," interrupted Scott.

"I don't feel comfortable proceeding until we get a hold of him," Sam quietly, yet firmly, countered.

But before an elder fight could break out, they heard the distinctive squeak of the front church door and the rapid footfalls of Pastor Griffith coming down the hallway.

Jonathan Griffith was forty-seven years old. He had been the pastor at Spring Valley for six years now, coming from a large church in California that he had planted earlier in his ministry career. He'd left it only when he'd felt he'd taken the plant as far as it could grow under his leadership. Across his years of ministry he had learned that he was best as an entrepreneurial innovator. He'd sensed in his heart that God was prompting him to turn it over to someone who had a different gift set and could, in his words, "take it to the next level."

What he'd anticipated when he accepted the position at Spring Valley was a lower stress opportunity to rejuvenate an existing church, sort of an entrepreneurial infusion into an existing community of believers without all the outsized demands that came with a startup church plant—like drafting a church constitution or dealing with zoning issues and building programs.

He had thought this church was ripe for change and that his entrepreneurial gift mix would be a nice match. Making the move to a smaller town and a smaller—although not small—church would be a win/win/win: a win for the church—due to his past experience, a win for him—less craziness and a win for the kingdom—

Or so he thought.

But instead of an easy experience, Pastor Griffith entered a culture that was equal parts poison and passion. This church had some great traditions and some horrible traditionalism. It had some great staff members and some who should have been dismissed years ago. It had some true elders and some, in the words he would only use with his wife, "imposters."

Pastor Griffith had sought to gently use the sail of salesmanship in elder meetings and the rudder of the pulpit to gently guide the church to a stronger place spiritually and structurally.

It had not worked.

"What's up gentlemen—and lady?" he said with a wink to Agnes as he walked into the room.

"You got my email?" Ryan asked timidly.

"And his phone call?" Pete asked with a smirk.

"Yes, to the email and no to the phone call," Pastor Griffith replied.

Sam seemed shocked. "I didn't think you checked your email on the weekends, Pastor Griffith."

"I don't. Everyone knows that I don't." His short, terse reply conveyed his displeasure.

"Then how did you find out about this meeting?" Sam asked.

"I got an emergency text about this emergency meeting from Agnes twenty minutes ago."

"iPhone," she said, holding hers up with an almost evil grin.

"Where's Chris?" Pastor Griffith asked, referring to the remaining missing elder.

"He couldn't make it," Scott said flatly.

"Guess he didn't get a phone call either," Pete said, inserting one last jab.

Ryan walked across the room, grabbed another metal chair for Pastor Griffith and opened it up with the horrible screeching sound metal chairs sometimes make. As uncomfortable as that sound was, it was not even close to the uncomfortable feeling in the room.

And the meeting had yet to officially begin.

2

UNQUALIFIED TO LEAD

Brothers and sisters, think of what you were when you were called. Not many of you were wise by human standards; not many were influential; not many were of noble birth. But God chose the foolish things of the world to shame the wise; God chose the weak things of the world to shame the strong. God chose the lowly things of this world and the despised things—and the things that are not—to nullify the things that are, so that no one may boast before him.

1 Corinthians 1:26-29

Ryan Coleman was your prototypical former high school quarterback youth pastor turned hipster "real pastor." It was obvious to everyone, but not stated by anyone, that he was being groomed by the elders to take over the church in the event that Pastor Griffith ever decided to move on. Although his square-rimmed glasses and soul patch concerned Scott years ago when Ryan was first hired as the youth leader, his strong seminary training and amazing organizational abilities relieved any latent concerns. Ryan always turned his budget in on time and always stayed within it. Once he had moved into the EP role he had "unflattened" the organization and put all the staff but Agnes under himself. And, of course, he submitted to Pastor Griffith's lead, while everyone else submitted to his.

Although Pastor Griffith was a much stronger preacher, Ryan used a lot of movie clips and funny stories to bolster his standing with the congregation. The teenagers liked it when he preached, anyway. He was tall, dark, good looking and hand-picked by Scott to be the future of Spring Valley.

Underneath his too-cool-for-school exterior was an ambition that was too-hot-to-handle. He knew that Pastor Griffith was tired of the politics of Spring Valley and had overheard his conversations with his wife on the phone in his office. There were at least three separate occasions in which he had eavesdropped the words, "I'll give it one more year," which Ryan took as a green light to his sooner, rather than later, pending position of power.

Over the years, he and Scott had developed an odd couple type of relationship. Like a cobra and mongoose, they did the dance at first. But they eventually settled into a weird partnership, Scott, the conservative middle-aged elder and Ryan the young, driven, hip and politically astute executive pastor.

Although Elder Scott and Pastor Ryan were different in many ways, they both were shockingly the same when it came to running the church. They called it "a sacred business." They would often quote 1 Corinthians 14:40 to others and each other, *"But everything should be done in a fitting and orderly way."*

This singular verse was the lens through which they viewed the entire church. From budgets to programs to pulpit to people, it was Ryan's job to dot the i's and Scott's job to cross the t's. And, when it came to this, they both excelled. Last year they had successfully added Jim Simpson to the elder board, further increasing their influence over the inner workings of the church. Jim could typically be relied upon to rubber stamp their policies, procedures and positions.

"Meeting come to order!" All the small talk stopped with that bellow from Scott.

"We are here to discuss the position of JC Davidson as the youth pastor here at Spring Valley and I propose we terminate him immediately," said Scott, mentally bracing himself for the storm that was about to hit.

"What!?!" yelled Pete. "You can't be serious!" His veins popped out from his flexed, muscular neck.

"I'm very serious," countered Scott, leaning toward Pete with a well-practiced scowl.

Standing to his feet Pete barked, "This is ridiculous! How dare you call a last minute emergency elders meeting because you have a vendetta against JC."

"It's not just me," said Scott. "I mean," he backpedaled, "well, I don't have a vendetta, but I do have several reasons he should be fired. And I'm not alone."

Still standing tall with his rugged hands clenched into giant fists frozen by his side Pete yelled, "Why couldn't this wait for our regular elders meeting? What's so important that we had to meet tonight?"

"I'll get to that, but—Ryan can back me up on this—it's serious," Scott pushed back.

"It is," affirmed Ryan.

"Was there some kind of moral failure with a teen or something?" asked Pete, backing down a bit.

"No, nothing like that, but it is serious," Ryan said coolly.

"What is it?" Pete demanded sitting back down in his chair, folding his rippling forearms across his chest.

"Well, there are many reasons, but the straw that broke the camel's back happened last night. I just learned about it this morning. That's why you got the email so late. It wasn't politics or a 'vendetta' but JC crossing an uncrossable line," said Scott. "But, before I talk about the proverbial final straw, I want to talk about the rest of the bale that's led up to this unfortunate meeting."

Pastor Griffith sat in stunned silence. He knew that both Ryan Coleman and Scott West had a personal grudge against JC ever since he hired him over their protests. He also knew that with an additional elder absent from this emergency meeting, there was no chance there would be enough votes present to oust JC tonight. Assuming these were all just trumped up charges—and he was ninety-nine percent sure they would be—there was no way that either he, Pete or Sam would cast a vote against JC. It would break out as a three-to-three tie. So if it came down to a vote, it would have to wait until a real elders meeting with everyone present and not this kangaroo court.

This was exactly the kind of politics that had been wearing on Pastor Griffith for the last few years. The machinery of ministry and politics of procedures was beginning to wear him down...and out. The rigid focus on SOPs—"Standard Operating Procedures"—had drowned out the SOS of the community around their church that so desperately needed God. Pastor Griffith had been waiting for God to turn the light from yellow to green so that he could step on the accelerator and leave the leadership of Spring Valley to those who so clearly wanted it.

"I've made a list of reasons for termination which I'll have Ryan pass out now," Scott instructed as Ryan complied. "Each of these reasons individually, could conceivably be dealt with, but collectively they paint a broader picture of rebellion in JC's heart that culminated last night."

"I don't see any fireable offence on the list," said Sam quietly.

"As I stated, in my opinion these are collectively fireable offences," countered Scott. "But the biggest reason is not on the list. I'll conclude with that one."

Pastor Griffith unknowingly rolled his eyes at Scott's penchant for the dramatic. Pete saw it and winked at him.

"Well, let's start at the top. Quite simply, JC is unqualified to lead in the role of youth pastor at Spring Valley. He has no formal seminary training and came straight from the construction business into the role of youth pastor here. No offense, Pastor Griffith, but if he hadn't framed your house and come to us with your strong personal endorsement, we would never have even given his resume a second look, let alone him," ranted Scott.

"To be honest, Scott," Pastor Griffith said, "he knows the Scriptures way better than me. I was astonished by his theological depth, as well. I think that in his case, his theology comes out of the vast amounts of time he spends in God's Word and it hasn't been filtered through a series of seminary professors. He actually has the book of Romans memorized word for word. I don't. Do you, Scott?" he asked with a slight smile on his face.

Pete tried to catch his laugh in his throat but it catapulted into the room. He was clearly enjoying the awkward moment.

Scott ignored the personal question and rebutted. "Well, this is no Bible quiz team, Pastor. This is the church. It takes organizers not verse nerds to lead. Without formal training in seminary how truly qualified could he be? I don't care how many books of the Bible he has memorized."

Before the pastor could counter, Scott continued, "On the other hand, take a look at Ryan over here. He went to seminary first and got his MDiv. We then hired him to be the youth pastor. Over the four years he was in that role here we saw the numbers grow. The families of this church were really happy with him. We even had families join our church because their kids loved the youth ministry so much. My own son, Chase, spent his entire youth ministry experience up until JC arrived, under Ryan's leadership. To be honest," Scott continued, "he misses Ryan as the youth pastor. He's always telling me how things have changed for the worse under JC's leadership."

Agnes pounded away on her laptop as Scott talked on and on. With his every word her finger pounds seemed to get louder and louder. She liked JC. She thought that every pastor should have, in her words, "a little dirt under their fingernails" before they go into ministry. And JC had plenty of it. His radical ways of ministry reminded her of a young Billy Graham who refused to do crusades that were not racially integrated back in the day when segregation was the norm. Her discontent with Scott's "agendetta" was getting louder with every click of the keys, until Sam gently put his hand on her shoulder and used his eyes to point to her keyboard. Agnes was old, but sharp. She got the message and dialed it back from a ten to a six on the laptop decibel scale. But that was the best she could do to contain her outrage.

Ryan took the baton from there. "Guys, it's not about me and my former role as youth pastor. And it's not just that he's unqualified to lead. It's that he chooses the unqualified to help him."

"He chose me," said Pete in a voice that sounded strangely like Clint Eastwood in *Dirty Harry*.

"I meant teens. He chooses unqualified teens to lead," said Ryan, backpedalling faster than a Mormon at Lee Strobel's house. "For instance, just two months ago, a girl named Maggie came to youth group after JC and Brandon, you know, Brandon Dempsey, the quarterback, bumped into her at a Starbucks—literally. I guess Brandon spilled his hot drink on her arm and she screamed in pain. JC knew that the coffee wasn't that hot, after all, Brandon had three-quarters hot coffee and one-quarter cool cream in his Venti cup. After apologizing profusely, JC saw that her coffee soaked sleeve was showing what was underneath her white shirt sleeve—cuts."

"Cuts?" asked Sam. "What's that?"

"Cutting is, well, it's hard to explain, 'cause it's hard to understand," Ryan said, floundering a bit, trying to find the right words. "Some teenagers today use a razor blade to cut themselves, most times on their torso or legs, but sometimes on their arms, too."

"Why would they do that?" asked a stunned Sam.

"Depression, self-hatred, anger, angst, sin, Satan or any combination of the above," responded Ryan with a true and sincere sadness in his voice. "It broke my heart to talk to these teens. Many of them don't even know why they cut. They just know that somehow that pain of the razor blade let's a deeper pain escape."

"So JC sees the cuts through her sleeve and then what," asked Scott impatiently, wanting Ryan to get back on point.

"Oh yeah, so he, Brandon and Maggie get into this conversation that lasted two hours. Brandon actually ended up missing his soccer practice as a result. But, at the end, she took the step of faith," said Ryan.

"Yeah, that's a firing offense, for sure," said Pete sarcastically.

"Nobody is saying that, Pete. Of course, that's a good thing. And her coming to youth group is a good thing, too," Ryan affirmed. "But she shouldn't be accepted into the leadership circle of youth group so quickly. Within four weeks, JC had her leading worship for the group."

Pete rose to JC's defense. "Maggie has a beautiful voice. She sings with reckless abandon, with eyes pointed upward, like nobody's in the room but her and God. It's like a perfume bottle that breaks open and fills the room whenever she sings."

"And you can still see the scars on her arms when she lifts her hands up to praise Him," Scott interrupted.

"Maybe," Pastor Griffith said calmly, turning his piercing blue eyes on Scott, "Maggie is non-verbally teaching our teens that they don't have to hide anything in the presence of God. We all have scars, Scott, and too many times we try to put on a fake front as we try to cover them up."

"Not literal ones!" Scott pushed back. "JC should make sure those scars are healed up before he puts her in a leadership position! He may be 'non-verbally' communicating to the teenagers that it's okay to cut as long as you have a good singing voice!"

Pete raised his voice again, "Scott, you should come to youth group sometime before you pass judgment."

"Well, Ryan's gone many times and he's told me what's going on there," Scott countered.

Pete shot back, "Yeah, he's come many times. I get the feeling he's been coming to make a mental list of all that he doesn't like about JC so he could report it back to you. Thank you for confirming that, Scott!"

"Pete," Sam interrupted, "we are the elders of this church and we do have a responsibility to make sure that things are being done by the book."

Sam's gentle rebuke calmed him down. But it was increasingly clear to Pete that Maggie was more qualified to lead worship than Scott was to lead the elder board.

3

MAGGIE

I'll never forget that day I bumped into JC and Brandon at the Starbucks. Who would have thought that a spilled cup of coffee could change the trajectory of your life?

Brandon had rushed off to get some napkins to help clean up the mess he'd made of my once white shirt, but JC's eyes were riveted to my arm. I realized that he could see what I'd been doing. Our eyes met and there was a depth of concern in his eyes that touched me. It was as though he instantly understood what had been going on deep down inside me.

When he asked me if he could pray for me, my response surprised even me. I am—I mean was—an agnostic, but for some reason I said "yes." And right there in the middle of Starbucks with his hand gently on my arm, he quietly prayed for me with an authenticity that touched me at my very core. With an "Amen!" from Brandon I was jerked back to reality, the reality that two strangers were praying for me in the middle of a busy Starbucks, the reality that I didn't really care how weird it looked and neither did they.

At that point, I was intrigued. When they asked me if we could sit down and talk awhile, I thought, what do I have to lose? After all, I was barely holding on just then, anyway.

So we talked. And the deeper the conversation got, the clearer it became that they cared about me and my pain.

I had never heard the gospel before then. I just had all these negative impressions about being judged by religious people and so my reaction to the whole churchy/God thing had always been "screw it."

At the root of it all, I think I really just felt like I was too stained and dirty whenever I thought about God type stuff. You see, I had some terrible things happen to me as a kid, and the older male "friend of the family" who was the perp had made me feel like "I'd asked for it."

Over time though, I thought I'd moved past what had happened to me. But I can see looking back now, that something deep inside me had been broken and never healed.

That and all the criticism and yelling at home sucked me into this vortex that spun a continual, ever louder message in my head: What a loser. You're worthless. You'll never measure up...What a loser. You're worthless. You'll never measure up... What a loser. You're worthless. You'll never measure up...

Before long, my unlovableness began to drown out everything else.

I looked older than I was, so by the time I was in middle school, I started hanging with older boys. And one thing led to another. I just liked their approval. God knows I never got any anywhere else.

I made some bad choices. And then to cover my mistakes, I did some things that were even more wrong.

By the summer before 9th grade, I started pharming and self-injuring. Both helped me temporarily escape the pain of my mess-ups. A few pills and a little slice would quiet down the voices in my head.

For a while.

But they always came back. And when the spinning vortex of self-loathing got too loud again, I'd pull out the pills and push in the blade. But increasingly, it took more and more to shut the screaming voices down. So I'd cut deeper. And get higher.

I knew things were spiraling out of control.

That's when I bumped into JC and Brandon at Starbucks and everything changed. Brandon told me about God, the real God. That this "God-man" lived and died for me. That He shed His blood for me, so that I was forgiven. For everything.

It all just clicked then. I'd gotten the part about being a "sinner" a long time ago. But this loving, forgiving God who reached down from heaven and offered new life? That WAS good news!

Forgiveness. Acceptance. Compassion. Love. What greater gifts could anyone offer me? I was all in.

They both invited me out to youth group and I went. Within a few weeks, JC overheard me singing in the crowd. I guess I was louder than the teen worship leader, even though he was armed with a microphone and a guitar. I didn't even realize that as I was singing so loud, tears were streaming down my face.

To be honest, I was just mesmerized by this whole Christianity thing, this great love story, and I couldn't help but sing and cry. Soon JC asked me to lead worship and it just seemed like I was drawn to it like a magnet. I just can't help but enter into His presence when I sing to Him, because He's everything to me. And I long to draw others into His presence, too, because it is such a beautiful place to be. So I have been leading worship in youth group ever since.

I'm not saying that I feel qualified to lead worship. I still struggle with plenty of stuff—negative crap that pours in and overwhelms me sometimes. And I admit there have even been a few instances since I've been saved that I've given in to the razor's edge. But now I feel like my life is on an upward trajectory. Words can't even begin to describe what the warmth of His love and forgiveness has done for me. Through the cross everything has changed. Through His shed blood I have been changed.

I guess like Pastor Griffith said a few weeks back, "God qualifies the unqualified."

That's me.

4

UNORTHODOX, INEFFECTIVE METHODS

From this time many of his disciples turned back and no longer followed him.

John 6:66

"Allow me to get back to my list here, gentlemen," Scott declared, jerking the steering wheel from Maggie's story back to his agenda. "Ryan was telling me about some of JC's unorthodox methods of ministry that don't seem to be working at all."

Before Ryan could begin to make his case, Pastor Griffith jumped in, "Funny, Ryan. You never mentioned anything about this to me."

"Well, Pastor," Ryan defended, "I know you're a busy man and I didn't want to distract you with this staff stuff. After all, the staff gives account to me," Ryan stated, flexing his org chart muscle a bit.

"And you give an account to me," said Pastor Griffith pointedly.

"And you both give an account to us," stated Sam, tired of the power plays. "Get to your point, Ryan."

"Thank you, Sam," Ryan responded. "My point is that when JC took over the youth ministry three-and-a-half months ago after I stepped into the executive pastor role, the youth ministry shrunk from 75 to 35 within a month."

"Is that true, Pete?" asked Pastor Griffith with a raised eyebrow and obvious concern.

"Well, yeah, I—I—I guess so," stuttered Pete. "But it's growing again."

"But it still hasn't reached the 75 mark again. Right, Pete?" asked Jim, entering the conversation for the first time.

"No, I guess not. But JC is always talking about the difference between a big youth group and a thriving youth group," Pete retorted.

"What do you mean?" asked Pastor Griffith.

"Yeah, what do you mean?" piped in Agnes. "Oops!" she blurted with her hand over her mouth, knowing that her curiosity, once again, had pinned her propriety to the mat.

"Well, JC put it this way," Pete said, "just because you have a big group doesn't mean that it's healthy. He used the example of big schools in New York City that have lots of students and lots of problems. He told us as a leadership team that we were going to start doing youth ministry in a different way—a way that is less about entertaining a crowd and more about engaging our group in a greater cause."

"What kind of cause?" asked Sam.

"THE Cause of making disciples, not just converts. THE Cause of loving God and loving each other, THE Cause of engaging 'sinners' on their turf and not just 'saints' on ours," Pete replied.

"Sounds exciting!" said Pastor Griffith. "But, if that's the case, then why did the youth group shrink?"

"Because JC told everybody that if they didn't want to be part of this bigger Cause and were there simply to be entertained, they might want to find a different youth group. He explained that while there's a place for fun and games—joy and camaraderie was how he put it—the Spring Valley youth group was about to become a serious training ground with a bigger purpose. He told the kids that when he was in construction he got paid to build something, to build something with his own hands. And in the same way, they were there to be built into disciples and to make disciples themselves. He made it clear that if they claimed to be Christians and weren't serious about this, then maybe this youth group wasn't going to be the best one for them. So many of them left," Pete said with a sigh.

"Including my own son, Chase," shot back Scott. "It's not that he doesn't want to be involved in a cause, but that's what mission trips are for. If we do a mission trip week in and week out, then all we are going to do is wear out our teenagers. And that's all that JC seemed to talk about, reaching out, going out. Chase said JC was always telling stories about people he'd shared the gospel with during the past week or invited to church and such. What about discipleship? What about pouring into the lives of the teenagers who call Spring Valley their home?"

"That's where you've got it mixed up, Scott," Pete interjected impatiently. "The teenagers who stayed on board started really growing in their faith as they engaged their friends, classmates, teammates and this community with the gospel. They pray and worship at youth meetings with an intensity that I've not seen even on Sunday mornings among the adults of this church. No offense, Pastor," he said glancing over at Pastor Griffith.

"None taken," the pastor responded.

"Although our youth group is back up to fifty students in attendance," Pete continued, "almost a third of them, including Maggie, came to faith through our teens at Spring Valley sharing their faith with their friends at school. And the youth ministry is electric with excitement, because now we're not just reading about what people who lived 2,000 years ago did for God, we're living it! We look around the room and see a dozen teenagers God has used us to reach with the gospel!"

Turning to face Scott directly, he concluded, "That's the difference between big and thriving."

"But what about JC's time in the office, Ryan?" asked Scott, shifting gears. "Didn't you tell me that you wish he spent more time actually working in the office?

"Yeah," Jim chimed in, "What does he do with his time, anyway?"

"He spends time with our teenagers at school almost every day!" Pete said heatedly, jumping in before Ryan could answer. "You all know that he meets kids for lunch at school in groups of two or three. He encourages them to invite their friends along. His purpose isn't so much to reach the lost kids himself, but to encourage and equip the Christian teens to share their faith with their friends at school. He's there to coach and encourage. I guarantee you he does more during those lunches than most youth leaders do in youth group in a month!"

"Regardless, he doesn't get paid to go out to lunch with everybody and their brother's friends at school. He gets paid to pastor the youth of Spring Valley," Scott said.

"Agreed," Ryan affirmed.

"That's exactly what he's doing," Pete protested. "He's just not doing it in the way that you did it, Ryan. As a youth volunteer under your youth ministry I saw your very conventional ways of ministering to the teenagers of Spring Valley. You used the games and curriculum and jumped through all the hoops and you grew a pretty big group. But I'd like to see where the graduating class from last year is now spiritually. As a matter of fact, I know—"

"Don't go there, Pete," Ryan said with a flash of anger. "There are national statistics that are plaguing every church. We were always trying to reverse the trends at Spring Valley of teens bagging their faith after high school. Maybe we should have tried something...," Ryan's voice trailed off.

"Unorthodox?" Pete inserted with a slight smile.

"Yes, I mean, no. I mean, nobody knows what the root problem is and I can guarantee you that just because JC does the bulk of his ministry on the outside of these four walls instead of on the inside, it won't necessarily mean his outcomes will be any better," Ryan said with a tone of defensiveness.

"And how can you guarantee that?" Pete asked. "Are you omniscient?"

Ryan sat there fuming, as Pete continued. "Guys, I'm a firefighter and every major firefighting innovation started as something unorthodox. And the biggest innovation in firefighting was not from our side, but the construction side. In 1871, The Great Chicago Fire broke out, leaving 100,000 homeless and 300 dead in the heart of Chicago. After that, the city of Chicago moved from wood buildings to masonry and steel as their primary building material. Now fires can be contained and put out before the building next door catches on fire."

"What's your point?" asked Jim.

"My point is that it took a disaster for the people of Chicago to change their methods and materials for building. I'd say the same kind of disaster is taking place in our youth ministries. We are building our teens with wood, hay and straw, not stone and steel. We are laying a foundation of sand, not rock. And as a result in many, many cases, their spiritual lives are being consumed by the world after they graduate from high school."

Pete continued his rant, "JC refuses to entertain. He refuses to use the typical materials and methods of youth ministry. He is helping to build teenagers into fully surrendered disciples and not just participants in a program."

"I don't get it, Pete," Scott said, "You mean JC is anti-fun?"

"No! He's not!" Pete corrected. "We are all having more fun than ever. But we're having fun for the best reasons, not just because we played games or had a pizza party—which we did last night, by the way—but because our Christianity is being applied to our real lives and not just our church lives. For the first time, our teens are getting a glimpse of what it actually looks like to overflow with the 'abundant life' the Bible talks about that comes from being all about following God."

"So does JC have a program that he runs inside the church or does he run it outside the church?" Sam asked with genuine confusion and concern.

"Yes!" Pete declared, frustrated that nobody seemed to understand. "JC has a great youth ministry program. Our meetings are organized and well thought out. But he views Wednesday night as 'the huddle' and the rest of the week as 'the game.' He said something once about Christianity being the only 'sport' that gets more excited about huddling up than running the plays."

Seeing that Pete was winning the point, Scott shot a zinger. "When Ryan and I talk about unorthodox we are not just referring to JC's penchant to spend too much time outside these four walls, but also his use of the youth ministry budget."

"What do you mean?" Sam asked. "Has there been some sort of misappropriation of finances?"

"Well, he did a pretty good job managing expenses the past three months. But, as we've pushed close to the end of the fiscal year, JC did something outside the boundaries." Everyone leaned in waiting to hear what Scott was going to say. "He gave the unused portion of the youth ministry budget to Compassion International."

"Good for him!" exclaimed Agnes, shooting a little fist in the air. "I love that ministry!"

Pastor Griffith turned to Agnes and said, "You do understand that we have a benevolence fund for that kind of giving, right? I don't know what the protocol is, but that does seem outside the boundaries of what should be done."

"Come on, Pastor!" Agnes pushed back. "Giving money to a ministry that feeds and ministers to poor children? If that's the worst they can come up with, then phooey on them."

"They?" asked Scott. "They are right here in front of you and, no offense, Agnes, but you are not in leadership here. You are here to take notes."

"Phooey," she whispered again under her breath, bringing her keyboarding decibel level back up to a ten.

"I'll talk to JC about this tomorrow," said Pastor Griffith. "At the very least, it's a breach of protocol."

"At the very least," affirmed Scott.

"Phooey," whispered Agnes.

5

MICHAEL

I've had enough of JC, believe you me. His scare tactics pretty much drove all of my friends away from youth group. His first week as YP and he gave this speech that pretty much boiled down to: "Get serious, or else..." Well honestly, he didn't scare me. I've heard enough of that kind of stuff from my dad to last a lifetime. He kinda bored me, actually. I was ready to laugh with my friends about him after youth group, but they weren't in the laughing mood. They thought JC's speech was ridiculous too, but once they talked to their parents about it, they got out scot-free and never came back.

Not my parents, though. I told my dad about that speech, how all of my friends were leaving. I pitched it like it was just the weird kids left, though that really isn't exactly true. And do you know what my dad did? He pulled out the standard "You're going to church, or else...We're pillars of the church... What would people say...blah, blah, blah...that kind of stuff." Sigh. So it's not my choice whether I go to youth group or not. My parents make me. They say church is important and people will talk if I don't go. It's ridiculous.

Yeah, I'm a Christian: born and raised. I've memorized a lot of verses through the years, but it doesn't mean I'm always confident that the Christian way is the only way to heaven. It might be the way for me, but who am I to push God on other people? And that's all that JC talks about, believe you me. That's all he seems to care about, too. I think maybe he's OCD.

Can't youth group just get together to have fun? Being a teenager is hard enough without having to have another thing to be guilted into doing. My parents guilt me into going to church. I really don't need church guilting me into ruining my social life and acting all judgmental.

There's enough pressure in my life already, believe you me. I don't need more from JC. With school, practice, college apps and everything else, I don't have time in my life for all of JC's little meetings. This God stuff is for Wednesday nights and Sunday mornings and that's more than enough. I'm a busy guy. I shouldn't have to be thinking about youth group stuff every day of the week. I've got homework, extracurricular activities and a social life. I've got all of those, and now if I want to hang out with my former "church friends" I've got to find more free time to do it in, since they no longer come out to youth group now that it's about more than pizza, dodgeball and hitting on hot girls.

And all those weird, borderline drug addicts who've started coming. I don't get how Brandon and some of the other jocks at youth group are being so nice to them. As far as I'm concerned, they've got no business at our church. They just don't belong here.

I'd leave if I could, believe you me, but that's not really an option with my parents. So I go, try not to make eye contact with anyone, sit down and zone out until the worst is over. Maybe I'll outlast JC and the group'll get rolling again without him around with his OCD, life-encompassing agenda.

6

DANGEROUS

The Son of Man came eating and drinking, and they say, "Here is a glutton and a drunkard, a friend of tax collectors and sinners." But wisdom is proved right by her deeds.

Matthew 11:19

"Well, it's getting late," Scott said, pushing the meeting forward. "Let's move on to the next item on the list."

"Yeah, I'm interested in this one," Pete said. "It just says 'dangerous.' Do you mean that JC is dangerous or that his way of doing ministry is?"

"Neither. His way of doing ministry is disruptive, for sure, but it's not him or his methods that concern me nearly as much as the caliber of teenager who is coming into this youth ministry as a result," replied Scott.

"Are you talking about what happened last night?" Pete said, his face once again turning red as his anger level rose.

"No. I'll get to that later. I'm talking about all the teenagers we're starting to see around here who look like they belong in a gang or a prison yard and not in the youth room at Spring Valley," Scott said coolly.

"They are looking pretty rough," Agnes chimed in. "I thought I was going to get mugged on the front doorstep of the church last Wednesday night when I dropped by to pick up that Chuck Swindoll book I've been reading during my lunch breaks. I wanted to give the book to a friend of mine that evening. Anyway, this big teenager who was wearing a black leather jacket and had a lip piercing stood at the door and seemed to be blocking my way into the church, but, at the last minute he said, 'Hello, welcome to Spring Valley,' and then opened the door."

"Yeah, that's Shane, he's part of the 'new' greeting team that JC put in place," said Ryan.

Everybody laughed.

"No, I'm serious," replied Ryan.

"Oh," was the collectively uncomfortable response.

"Let me explain," Pete said, rushing in defensively. "First off, you're not being fair in your characterization of the new kids joining the group. It's a real mix. We have all kinds of kids, jocks, band kids and nerds, the whole gamut of your typical high school social groups. But Shane, the kid in question here was indeed in a gang up until last month. He came to faith when Maggie shared the Good News with him at school."

"Shouldn't we maybe wait a bit," Sam responded, "until he grows in his faith and gets used to the way we do things at Spring Valley before we put him in a position of leadership?"

"He's part of the *greeting* team." Pete shot back, "I wouldn't exactly call it a position of leadership. It's a position of service—"

"But even then—" Sam interrupted.

"Even then, what?" Pete interrupted back.

Scott and Ryan sat back in their metal chairs happy that for once it was Sam, not them, tangling with the big fireman.

"I know of a certain guy in the Bible," Pete continued, "who was radically converted on the road to Damascus. He was transformed from the persecutor of the church to the preacher of the gospel in about 2.3 seconds. Gentlemen, I wonder if we're failing to really believe in the transformational power of the gospel to change lives. If we really believe in the power of the gospel, then why wouldn't we put every new believer in a position of service as soon as possible? And unleash them immediately to share the Good News with all their friends?"

Sensing that Sam was losing the argument, Scott piped in. "Maybe so, it's just that these new believers need to be discipled and coached first before we put them in positions of influence."

Pete responded with a verbal machine gun. "What, like the woman at the well, who moments after her conversion influenced her whole town with the gospel? Like Zacchaeus who went from notorious sinner to notorious philanthropist upon descent of a fig tree? Like—"

"Stop!" yelled Scott, the veins on his not-so-muscular neck bulging in outrage. "We are not in the early church and you are not an apostle! We are at risk of being sued if some kid sells drugs to another kid in youth group and he overdoses.

We are in a litigious society and bad things could happen to this whole church if we don't address this. Quite simply, JC has got too many of the promiscuous, drug using crowd in the youth ministry. Last week Ryan caught the Franklin boy smoking a joint in the parking lot."

"Jared Franklin?" asked Jim.

"Yep."

"What happened?" Jim pressed.

"I guess one of the new kids that someone brought out to youth group gave it to him," Scott replied.

"That is definitely unacceptable," Pastor Griffith replied.

"To JC's credit, he addressed it right afterwards with all the kids," Ryan said. Scott cleared his throat uncomfortably in an effort to get Ryan's attention and refocus him back on JC's shortcomings.

Ryan ignored him and forged ahead. "And I agree that we need to do everything we can to prevent this from happening in the future."

"I agree," Pete chimed in. "But we can't have it both ways."

"What do you mean?" asked Sam.

"We can't be faithful to God's command to make disciples of everyone, without taking the risk of getting our teens exposed to some of this stuff," Pete said.

"We are here to protect these teenagers!" Scott objected.

"No!" Pete replied. "We are here to prepare these teenagers! If you really want to prepare your teenagers for college, for life after youth group, then you better get used to the fact that they'll be around drugs, alcohol, secular worldviews, promiscuous sex and all sorts of other vices once they go off to college or the work force. Unless, like some families in our church, our goal is to throw up the fortress walls and keep them in a Bible bubble all of their lives."

Agnes giggled out loud, knowing exactly which families at Spring Valley Pete was referring to in his rant.

"If we can't help equip them to face these challenges now," Pete continued, "then how will they face them when we aren't around to smack the drugs out of their hands?"

Sensing that once again Pete was winning the argument, Scott went straight for the jugular, "Listen guys, I know that we've already lost three families over this sort of stuff. The Hendersons, Kellys and Jacksons. One of those 'Bible bubble' couples, who shall remain unnamed, funded 5% of our overall church budget last year and now they are gone because of, in their words, 'the new element in the youth group.' "

"What's your point?" asked Pete.

"It's simply this," Scott answered, "This year was tight financially anyway. If we continue to lose tithing families because we want to bring the outcasts in, then we are going to be in some serious financial trouble come next fiscal year."

"So," Pastor Griffith said with a tone of concern, "What you are implying is that if JC and his core crew of teenagers continue to reach the lost we will lose money as a church and, therefore, we should stop reaching the lost?"

Scott backed up a bit, "Well, no. Of course we want them to reach the lost, but our church is in an upper middle class area. So then why do the teenagers that Spring Valley seems to be attracting look so dangerous? Those who go to a church should be comprised of the demographic of its socio-economic community."

"Who told you that, the church attendance fairy?" asked Pete angrily.

Agnes laughed so hard she snorted. Even Pastor Griffith and Sam couldn't contain their amusement and smiled.

"Think about the demographic of the first disciples," Pete added heatedly, "stinky fishermen, greedy tax collectors and slutty prostitutes. How do you like that demographic?"

"Quit trying to spiritualize everything!" Scott shouted back.

It got quiet as Scott's flash of anger cooled to embarrassment. In the core of his soul, he knew that it was actually his job as an elder to spiritualize everything. Was he kicking against the goads? A twinge of doubt crossed his mind briefly, but seconds later he shook off the glimmer of conviction and said in a neutral voice, "I just think we need to be careful with those kinds of kids."

Sensing Scott's de-escalation, Pete reciprocated and scaled back the emotional charge in his voice a few degrees. "Scott, it's 'those kinds of kids' that, generally speaking, already know they're sinners and they're attracted to the grace that flows from the life of JC and the students and adult volunteers he has trained."

Scott retorted, "That's all well and good but—"

Pastor Griffith interrupted, "That is all well and good—very good. But I do have a question for you, Pete."

"What's that, Pastor?" Pete asked.

In an effort to further soften the tone of the conversation, Pastor Griffith asked calmly, "If JC is so committed to getting Christian teenagers to share their faith, then why is he using youth group as an outreach? Shouldn't he be training teenagers to engage their own friends at their own schools?"

"He is!" Pete answered. "Actually most of the youth group meetings are not designed to be outreach meetings. Sure, he always gives the gospel just in case somebody there has never heard it. But, many of these teenagers come into youth group already saved."

"Really?" Pastor Griffith asked.

"Yes!" Pete responded with a broad smile. "Most of the new teenagers who come have already heard and responded to the gospel. I'd guess about 60% of the new kids became Christians through another teen in the group before they ever came to youth group."

"Wow! That's pretty impressive!" the pastor admitted. "If that happened with the adults in our church we'd call that a revival!"

"Yes, we would," Sam affirmed in his understated but authoritative way.

Seeing he was losing ground again, Scott threw another get-back-to-point look at Ryan and said, "But I know for a fact that once a month JC does have an outreach meeting, as he did last night. And it's at these outreach meetings that I feel things get a bit out of control."

"I don't understand. Are you saying kids get too rowdy? Do they break things, put holes in the wall, stuff like that?" Sam asked.

"No, I'm saying that JC lets teenagers have a free-for-all discussion about a certain, pre-chosen, usually intensely controversial subject," Ryan inserted.

"What's wrong with that?" Pastor Griffith asked.

"Well, you have teenagers from vastly different worldviews sharing their opinions about subjects like sex, music, drugs and stuff like that," Ryan said.

"But JC never affirms their answers, just their honesty." Pete defended. "He always circles around to what the Bible says at the end and he always shares the gospel or has a teen share it."

"Yeah, he does it in a ten minute segment of a 90 minute meeting, at the very end," Ryan shot back.

"That's all it takes," Pete said. "And, once again, it's this 'dangerous' form of youth ministry that is more about preparing our Christian teens for what they'll face in and after high school, than pretending like that raw, real, gritty world out there doesn't exist. Our kids who go to public schools hear the f-bomb dozens of times each day. They see drugs changing hands in the school parking lot. "

Everyone was silent, so Pete continued, "So JC chooses to address it head on. It's that kind of raw honesty that made Shane want to participate in youth group and greet people at the door. He wanted to be the first face that people saw so they didn't mistake Spring Valley for a typical close-minded church. Because we're not that. Right?"

"Right," Agnes said under her breath.

"Amen." Pastor Griffith added in a whisper.

7

SHANE

I'm the last guy you'd expect at church. I guess I'm the last guy I'd expect at church. There's a rage that's been burning inside me since I was twelve years old. To be honest, I don't know why.

Maybe it's because my dad used to beat me up.

Maybe it's because my mom was too weak to fight back, weak because of the alcohol, weak because she always got beat up, too.

I don't know how, but somehow, in seventh grade I got labeled "bully" and for some reason, I liked it. There was something about being the kid others would cringe from when I walked down the hall. It gave me a feeling of power.

When I'd hit somebody, I didn't see my dad's face, but I think I felt his rage coursing through my veins. To add insult to serious bodily injury, I was way bigger than my classmates. Even kids two grades ahead were afraid of me.

Something about the weak kids, the effeminate boys... yeah, you know which ones I'm talking about, used to really make me mad.

My dad used to call me a sissy all the time. Maybe that was the trigger for my rage toward them. I don't know.

All I know is that all that changed when Maggie entered my life. Sure, before that day, she sometimes sat at the other end of the empty cafeteria table I'd parked myself down at. I just figured she was another troubled girl. Everybody knew she was a cutter. Everyone assumed she was a slut.

But something changed when JC and Brandon "baptized" her with coffee in the Starbucks that day. She came to school that week beaming. I noticed it once in the hallway and, to be honest, I thought she was on amphetamines or something. But I knew something was up when I was in the cafeteria eating lunch all by myself...like I did every day. She just walked up with her food tray, sat down right next to me and said, "How are you?"

I flashed a look of rage in her direction and she just flashed a smile back. I'll never forget her putting her hand on my shoulder and whispering, "Can I talk to you about something?"

The next twenty minutes were a blur. I just knew that when she was done my eyes were salty and my cheeks were wet. Even "the sissies" were pointing in my direction and whispering to each other.

Maggie introduced me to a dad who would never beat me, who sacrificed his own son to call me his. And I was changed.

My bullying stopped that day. I dropped out of the gang of troublemakers I used to hang out with. I'm not saying I turned perfect that day, but something inside me just totally changed.

So when Maggie invited me to youth group, I gladly said "yes." Hearing JC talk about God gave me such a feeling in my soul that I don't think I can explain it. And the singing to God was great, too. I especially love to watch Maggie sing—scars and all.

I'm still working on forgiving my dad, but as Pete told me (I love that guy!), if God can forgive me for my sins, then I can forgive my dad for his.

Whatever is going on, I like it. I have hope for the first time. The rage in my soul is fleeing the scene.

8

EXTREME

Very early in the morning, while it was still dark, Jesus got up, left the house and went off to a solitary place, where he prayed. Simon and his companions went to look for him, and when they found him, they exclaimed: "Everyone is looking for you!"

Mark 1:35-37

"Can we take a break?" asked Agnes.

A confused look flashed across Scott's face.

"I have to go potty," she clarified.

"Me too," said Pete. "Let's reconvene in 10 minutes."

It was already 10:30 p.m. A simple glance at the remaining agenda points left everyone thinking the same thought. In all likelihood, this meeting would be going past the strike of midnight.

Pete, Scott and Ryan ended up at the urinal wall. To break the awkward silence in the who-goes-first-moment, Pete asked Ryan, "So I see that 'extreme' was next on your list. What's that all about?"

Scott interrupted quickly, "Shouldn't we just wait until we're all situated back in the room to continue the meeting?"

"It's okay, Scott," Ryan responded, "we're just talking here."

"Well, not *just* talking," Pete said with a laugh.

Even Scott smiled at that one.

Ryan continued the conversation as he walked over to wash his hands, "It's just that JC seems overzealous in everything he tackles. He has an almost cult-like excessiveness to everything he does."

"Cult-like?" asked Pete. "Seriously?"

"Well, take for instance the way he prays," responded Ryan. "JC can't just pray and leave it alone. He prays all day throughout the day. He blurts out spontaneous prayers in the middle of meetings, even sometimes gives the rest of us these little word picture lessons about God—even with the senior pastor! I mean, I don't even presume to do that and I've been around here four years longer than he has and been to seminary to boot. And there's a matter-of-factness to his prayers that borders on the disrespectful, in my opinion."

"Yeah," Pete responded, "I've heard him busting out in one of his spontaneous prayers in the middle of announcements once. The kids thought he had lost his mind. Two months ago when we did our winter retreat we couldn't find him on Saturday morning and he was supposed to teach the lesson then. He told us that he went on a prayer walk and got caught up in praying for us all."

Scott and Pete joined Ryan at the sinks as Scott affirmed, "Yeah, that seems kind of overzealous to me."

Ryan jumped back in, continuing his litany, "And, Pete, you should see him when he actually is at work. He probably spends only half of his time in the office. Often he's walking around the building on some kind of prayer walk. He's usually moving his lips as he prays, so he looks kind of crazy. I can't help but see him from my office window. I've actually had people from the neighborhood ask me about the crazy man who walks around the building all the time. I practically cringe inside every time I have to tell them that he's our youth pastor."

"He does talk about prayer all the time," Pete acknowledged. "He told me that this is how he prepares for his lessons. He prays for the teenagers in the group by name. He prays for the schools they go to. He prays for the unity, focus and transformation of Spring Valley. He prays for the elders and pastors at this church, including you and Scott, every day, by name."

"Yeah, well, that's good..." Ryan said awkwardly, his voice trailing off into an uncomfortable silence. But Ryan knew enough to keep his mouth shut at this point since he couldn't honestly say the same about praying regularly for JC. He'd spent more time plotting against him with Scott than interceding for him with God.

"He actually told me that this is how he prepares his lessons," Pete continued. He walks around the building and prays over the passage he's going to talk on and asks God for insights."

"Ah, that's why he carries his Bible with him as he prays and looks down at it from time to time," responded Ryan. "Come to think about it, maybe that's why he stops and jots things down from time to time as he walks. He's writing insights down."

"I guess," Pete agreed. "And you thought he was crazy."

"I suppose maybe there might be some method to the madness," Ryan responded.

As they moved into the hallway Scott said bluntly, "Again, nobody is against JC praying but, to be honest we don't pay him to pray. We pay him to work. He can pray on his own time."

Ryan paused and wondered if he really agreed with Scott on this particular point. He couldn't help but flash back to his required seminary reading of the Andrew Murray and E.M. Bounds books on prayer. He remembered the utter conviction he'd felt reading them. As a matter of fact, there was one quote from E.M. Bounds he had committed to memory back in those days:

> What the Church needs today is not more machinery or better, not new organizations or more and novel methods, but men whom the Holy Ghost can use—men of prayer, men mighty in prayer. The Holy Ghost does not flow through methods, but through men. He does not come on machinery, but on men. He does not anoint plans, but men—men of prayer.[1]

In spite of the non-egalitarian nature of this quote, it had inspired him when he was in seminary. But the demands of his MDiv program—the volume of reading, the exegesis of texts, the multiple drafts of his thesis paper—they'd all blocked this aspiration from becoming a reality in his life.

It crossed Ryan's mind that maybe part of what irritated him about JC's approach to prayer was how it served as a constant reminder of his own failure to achieve this divine ambition of being a prayer warrior. Did he see in JC's prayer life something of what he had actually once aspired to himself?

Ryan tamped those feelings down and girded back up for the meeting. He was letting his guard down and allowing JC's persuasive persona to cloud his judgment. For the good of the youth group and the good of the church, he had to stiffen his resolve.

But he also realized it would be best to cross "extreme" off of the list of reasons to fire JC. As Pete went down the hallway to grab a drink of water from the fountain Ryan turned to Scott and said, "I'm dropping this one off of the agenda list. I don't know if a person can be too extreme in prayer."

"Come on, Ryan," Scott retorted, "man up. Don't turn all touchy-feely spiritual on me now—"

"I'm not taking him on for praying too much, Scott. And that's final," Ryan said bluntly under his breath. "Let's move on to the next item on the list. It's a lock anyway."

"Okay," said Scott, reluctantly, as they pushed the door of the room back open to reengage the difficult meeting.

9

DISRESPECTFUL

In the temple courts he found men selling cattle, sheep and doves, and others sitting at tables exchanging money. So he made a whip out of cords, and drove all from the temple area, both sheep and cattle; he scattered the coins of the money changers and overturned their tables. To those who sold doves he said, "Get these out of here! How dare you turn my Father's house into a market!" His disciples remembered that it is written: "Zeal for your house will consume me."

John 2:14-17

Once Pete came in the door, wiping the water dripping from his cheek off with his hand, Pastor Griffith reopened the conversation by saying, "It looks like 'extreme' is next on your checklist here, Ryan. What's that about?"

"Pastor," Ryan said, glancing up at the standard church issue clock hanging above the doorframe. "'I've just decided that it'd be best if we left this one alone and skipped on to the next point."

"Good call!" Pete affirmed as he walked by Ryan to take his seat, squeezing Ryan's shoulder on the way back to his own spot at the table.

Ryan managed a half smile, while Scott's face displayed a self-confident smirk.

"So what I want to get to next is the disrespectful nature of JC's one and only sermon here at Spring Valley," Ryan stated flatly.

"The one on parenting?" asked Jim.

"Yes," Ryan responded abruptly.

"That was awesome!" Pastor Griffith replied. "He was practically flipping pews over that morning! You could literally feel the tension when he told the parents of the teenagers in the group that he wasn't there to spiritually suckle their children and observed that many of them had relegated, delegated and abdicated their spiritual responsibility to him, an unmarried ex-carpenter with no children of his own."

"I think that's when we lost the Kelly family, by the way," Jim inserted. "They literally stormed out of the service during the closing song and haven't been back since."

"Pastor," Scott said, bypassing Jim's remark, "I think it was disrespectful. How dare a thirty year old who's never been married lecture moms and dads to spiritually train their own teenagers. That's what we pay him for!"

Pastor Griffith shot back, "I don't agree, Scott." Reaching over and grabbing Sam's Bible he continued, "Listen to what it says here in Deuteronomy 6:6-9,

> *"These commandments that I give you today are to be on your hearts. Impress them on your children. Talk about them when you sit at home and when you walk along the road, when you lie down and when you get up. Tie them as symbols on your hands and bind them on your foreheads. Write them on the doorframes of your houses and on your gates."*

All JC was doing was giving them a much needed reminder that it is their job, not his, to live out Deuteronomy 6 in their own homes," Pastor Griffith affirmed.

Pete and Agnes silently nodded their agreement.

"But when he called them out for being too consumeristic, for going to church for their own benefit and social status and for not being the church at home in front of their kids, he was making a sweeping judgment on their homes which he had no right to do," Ryan continued.

"Yeah, he maybe could have toned that part down a bit," Pastor Griffith admitted. "I can see how some people could feel like that was a bit over the line."

"He was dead on," Agnes commented, again inserting her thoughts into the meeting uninvited. "I see so many Lexus and BMWs in the church parking lot every Sunday morning. I can't help but wonder, if these moms and dads put their focus on God, His kingdom and the spiritual development of their own kids, maybe we wouldn't be seeing the massive exodus of teenagers from the church after they graduate."

Momentarily forgetting that she wasn't supposed to be contributing to the discussion, Scott responded, "That's a bold statement, Agnes."

"Well, when I was a teenager, my mom and dad weren't concerned about making a bunch of money and buying a fancy car," she said, continuing to vent her opinionated perspective. "As a matter of fact, when it came to me, they weren't nearly as concerned about me being happy or making the honor roll as they were about me being a woman of God. We didn't have youth pastors back then, because we didn't need youth pastors back then. We had parents that led family devotionals and prayed with us and for us."

"So you're saying we shouldn't have a youth pastor at all, Agnes?" asked Pastor Griffith.

"Not at all. That was then, this is now. Lots of families in our community are broken, I would say even in our own church. And even when the dads are home, many of them are disengaged from their own children—and the moms aren't much better," Agnes continued. "I think we need youth pastors like JC to step up and challenge these consumeristic parents to do their jobs. And then to help them do it. I know that every week JC has me send out a list of questions via email to the parents at Spring Valley who have teens in our group. These questions are based on his lesson that week. They are designed to get parents talking about spiritual things with their own teens."

"But what about teenagers in the group who don't have parents who would ever do this, like the Shane's and Maggie's?" asked Sam.

"That's where we come in," said Pete.

"We?" asked Sam, "the elders?"

"No. 'We' the adult volunteers," answered Pete. "That's why JC did such a hard push that Sunday morning both on getting parents to step up and adult sponsors to step into that role of spiritual mentor to the teens."

"I'm even thinking about doing it," said Agnes. "JC approached me after the service that day and told me that he thought I'd be a great candidate to serve in the youth ministry."

Scott gingerly asked, "But aren't you too, well, um...."

"Old?" asked Agnes. "Not according to JC! He told me that teens are looking for someone who loves God, loves them and is authentic. I told him that, at the very least, I had the third one in the bag. And he said he could tell that the first two were true for me, as well."

"That's for sure," said Pastor Griffith with a smile. Turning to Ryan and Scott, he continued, "Sorry guys, but you can cross that one off of your list, too. What you thought of as disrespectful was just the hard truth that parents need to step up and adults need to step in. If anything, I should have been the one to preach that sermon, not JC. After all, I am the pastor of this church."

But Scott wasn't willing to let the point go. There were bigger issues at stake here and he was adamant they be addressed. "Okay, then let me acknowledge the elephant in the room. We all know that the Kellys are the ones who were initially offended by the new and dangerous 'clientele' in the youth group. And they ultimately decided to walk out as a result of JC's 'bold' sermon. And with their exit, our church budget took a $75,000 annual hit."

Ryan momentarily found his backbone once again and pushed back against Scott's point. "Although I still think JC was disrespectful from the pulpit to the parents here at Spring Valley, I have to disagree that we should always tone down the sermons preached from our pulpit because they might offend our major donors in some way. It feels like we would be kissing up to our biggest donors so that they keep giving."

"That's not what I'm saying," Scott defended himself.

"I think it is," said Pete bluntly.

"Well, we are going to have to agree to disagree then," Scott said abruptly, while giving Ryan the evil eye of betrayal. "It's time to move on to the next agenda item."

Down deep inside he knew that he still had the upper hand—even if the rest of them at the table were naïve, business-illiterate idealists. Some things were more than obvious and the disaster of losing major donors like the Kelly family was undisputedly one of those things.

10

MARY AND CRAIG KELLY

"We don't know who this JC thinks he is, but his confrontational ways drove us straight out of Spring Valley Church. He claims to be implementing some kind of radical new form of youth ministry, but it just feels pushy and judgmental to us. The idea—telling us parents to back off on the outwards signs of 'success' and be more involved in the spiritual development of our kids. Just because he's a former manual laborer, he has it out for those of us who have made something of ourselves and now enjoy displaying the hard-earned fruits of our labor. He should show more respect for those of us who actually have our act together and are leading successful lives.

After all, we hire an architect to design changes to our house, we hire a tax accountant to take care of our taxes, we hire a nanny to take care of our kids and we hire a gardener to take care of our yard. It's the same thing. We expect the youth pastor we hire—since we basically fund a huge chunk of the church's budget with our donations—to take care of the God part of our kids' lives. It's his job, for heaven's sake.

Our son was doing fine when Ryan was the youth pastor. He was even part of the worship band because he has such a beautiful singing voice. Then a few weeks ago he got ousted from leading worship by Maggie, a brand new Christian. According to our son, she's a cutter. The last thing this youth group needs is a novice Christian who leads worship and is known for what she does with a razor blade.

All that was bad enough, but then when JC preached that sermon lecturing all the parents, we just said, "Enough is enough." We don't have to stand for this. There are plenty of other churches in this town who would be more than happy to bend over backwards to have us and our generous donations.

And the sooner Spring Valley figures out that they have a disruptive, disrespectful, loose cannon of a youth pastor on their hands, the better for everyone. We're really doing the church a favor by getting up and walking out. It'll get their attention and they'll wise up sooner this way. After all, there's no doubt about it, money talks.

11

PLAYS FAVORITES

After six days Jesus took with him Peter, James and John the brother of James, and led them up a high mountain by themselves.
Matthew 17:1

Standing up to stretch, Pastor Griffith cracked his knuckles and his neck and said, "Let's get through this last agenda item so we can get home and get to bed."

"Do you want to finish the list or should I?" asked Scott, his voice conveying a hint of his disappointment at Ryan's retreat from their pre-agreed stance on the last two agenda points.

"I'll do it, Scott," Ryan assured him.

Sensing that Ryan's loyalty might be fracturing, Pete encouraged him by saying, "Yeah, you do it, Ryan."

"Okay, and this is a pretty serious one, in my opinion," Ryan said. Once again Scott's smirk spread across his face. "JC plays favorites."

"What do you mean by that?" Sam asked.

"He has a core of teenagers that he gives preferential treatment to because they, in his opinion, have a higher level of commitment to God and 'THE Cause' he has given them to reach their schools with the gospel," answered Ryan.

"So, what's wrong with that?" Pete asked.

"Well, when I was the youth leader here, my philosophy was to love all the kids equally and to pour into them equally no matter where they were on the spiritual continuum," Ryan responded.

"So more of a communistic approach to spiritual maturity?" Agnes deadpanned with only a ghost of a smile. Even Scott and Jim choked back a laugh with that one.

"No, not at all," Ryan assured them. "More of an approach that let the kids know they were equally loved, no matter how they acted or where they were at. I wanted them to know that there's nothing that they can do to make me, or God, for that matter, love them more or less."

"I don't think with JC it's a matter of love, but a matter of leadership," Pete responded.

"What do you mean?" Sam asked, leaning forward in his metal chair.

"Well," Pete said, "I know JC is praying for all the teenagers. There have been a few times I've walked into his office to find him actually shedding tears as he looked at pictures of them posted on the wall and prayed for them. He is always open to talking to them if they need him and he pours his life blood out into his weekly lessons. But he's also made it very clear that he simply cannot humanly invest his life into every teenager at Spring Valley, after all there are fifty of them now and growing!"

"So," Scott interrupted, trying to pretend like he was being spontaneous, "what you are saying is that JC basically invests in the kids he likes and avoids the ones he doesn't?"

"No!" Pete said, "it's not a popularity contest or about him liking one kid more than another. It's about the reality that one youth leader can only pour into the lives of so many teenagers on a serious investment level."

"So how many teenagers does JC invest in?" asked Jim skeptically.

"I don't know, there's eleven or twelve students who show up to the weekly leadership gatherings. I'm not exactly sure they should be called 'meetings'—they're more like life-on-life discipling times, where they talk candidly about who God is, how to follow Him, God's heart for the lost, how to reach others with the gospel, how to disciple others—important stuff like that, " answered Pete.

"So, what you're telling us is that, although we pay him to lead the entire youth ministry, he is only pouring his life into, at best, twelve students?" asked Scott, sensing blood in the water for the first time in awhile.

"Well, um...," Pete stumbled momentarily. "JC's philosophy is that if he can pour his life into a handful of ultra-committed teens, then they will actually influence the rest of the group exponentially. But if he tries to pour himself into the whole group, his efforts will be diluted to the point of ineffectiveness. It's like me trying to fight a fire with a water sprinkler, rather than a high pressure hose."

Pastor Griffith flipped open his iPad and started searching for something while Pete continued, “Again, it’s not a matter of love, but of leadership. JC is looking for high-will, raw-skill teenagers to pour into so that they can pour into others and so on, you know, make disciples who make disciples.”

“So, how does JC choose who is a part of this leadership team?” Ryan probed suspiciously.

“Pure willingness and commitment to God and THE Cause. That’s it,” answered Pete.

“Explain more what you mean by ‘THE Cause’?” Sam interjected. “You’ve used that term more than once tonight, Pete.”

“It’s the cause in Matthew 28:19 to *‘go and make disciples of all nations’* and JC is convinced that it doesn’t start across the seas, but across the classroom aisle at school,” Pete replied, gaining his stride and almost preaching. “That’s why if you go into his office you’ll see a map of our community and red boundary lines from I-70 to 80th Avenue and Sheridan Boulevard to Ward Road. That’s what we call our ‘Cause Turf.’ Our goal is to mobilize teenagers at every one of the high schools and middle schools in this area who will make disciples who make disciples until every teenager on these school campuses hears the gospel from a teenager they know. And until every teen who responds to the gospel is plugged into a solid church.”

“Our church you mean, right?” asked Scott.

“Come on, Scott,” Pete pushed back, “do you really think that Spring Valley teens can reach every teen in our city? It’s going to take a gospel-centered movement that’s drenched in prayer and focused on results to make this happen. It's going to take all hands on deck! JC has just joined the local youth leader's network and is really praying about how to cast this vision to them. His hope is to start by just getting them to pray on behalf of the schools in this community. He is convinced that if they really learn to intercede for this community, all of the evangelism and discipleship will spill out of that heart for the lost."

Sensing the need to take a different tack, Ryan shifted in his chair and tried to move the discussion back to how JC picks students to lead. "I'm still having a hard time justifying sheer passion as the sole qualifier for leadership in the group."

"Yes, I agree," Scott inserted forcefully. "Shouldn't consistency in attendance, Bible knowledge and skill play a role?"

"They sure don't hurt," Pete agreed. "But without passion and, of course, commitment, then all of that other stuff turns into legalism. We end up with—in your words, Scott,—the 'verse nerds' ruling the roost. Those who don't know any lost people and aren't willing to get out in the gritty street because they would rather just continually talk about their Christianity with each other than actually get dirty by rubbing shoulders with the unreached."

Agnes, who had reached over and grabbed Sam's well worn Bible while Pete was talking, interrupted him, "Reminds me of this passage in Luke 14:26-33,

> *"If anyone comes to me and does not hate father and mother, wife and children, brothers and*

> *sisters—yes, even their own life—such a person cannot be my disciple. And whoever does not carry their cross and follow me cannot be my disciple.*
>
> *"Suppose one of you wants to build a tower. Won't you first sit down and estimate the cost to see if you have enough money to complete it? For if you lay the foundation and are not able to finish it, everyone who sees it will ridicule you, saying, 'This person began to build and wasn't able to finish.'*
>
> *"Or suppose a king is about to go to war against another king. Won't he first sit down and consider whether he is able with ten thousand men to oppose the one coming against him with twenty thousand? If he is not able, he will send a delegation while the other is still a long way off and will ask for terms of peace. In the same way, those of you who do not give up everything you have cannot be my disciples."*

"Sounds like passion and commitment were the requirements to be a part of the original leadership team to me," said Agnes, closing the Bible with a thud and handing it back to Sam with a wink.

"No offense, Agnes," Scott pushed back, "but JC's leadership team, from what I can see, is more like the island of misfit toys than the early disciples."

"Really?" interrupted Pastor Griffith looking up from his iPad. "Don't you remember that sermon I preached last summer on the disciples? Most of them had probably been overlooked by other rabbis after having failed their interviews with them. That's why many of them had learned their father's trade. They had most likely been passed over by other rabbis and had resigned themselves to collecting taxes or fish or whatever. But then a rogue rabbi who likely saw a passion for God boiling underneath chose them, trained them and mobilized them for, well, THE Cause."

"He chose the foolish things to confound the wise!" Sam said more forcefully than his usual calm, reserved tone.

"Not only is JC's approach of choosing high-will, raw—what did you call it again, Pete?" Pastor Griffith turned and asked.

"High-will, raw-skill, Pastor," replied Pete.

"That's it!" agreed Pastor Griffith. "Not only is that approach Biblically solid, but it's culturally relevant."

Looking down at his iPad he said, "I want to read you an interesting statistic I just came across in an article I was reading last week. It strikes me that it's pertinent to this discussion. Here it is,

> Researchers at (RPI) Rensselaer Polytechnic Institute have found that when just 10 percent of the population hold an unshakable belief, their belief will always, eventually be adopted by the majority of the society.[2]

"Do you realize what this means?" Pastor Griffith continued. "If you can get 10 percent of a youth group on fire for God, then they will influence the entire group!"

Pete, quickly grasping the implications of the research, added excitedly, "And what's true of a youth group is true of a church, a community and a nation! Just imagine the impact that can ripple out from a committed core!"

"Yes!" agreed Pastor Griffith. "If we can get 10 percent of our congregation 'all in' for THE Cause, then our whole church can capture the vision. And if we can get our whole church on fire for THE Cause, we can affect our whole community and so on!"

"So," Ryan said, circling back around to the original topic, "It's okay to play favorites in your opinion, Pastor?"

"To be honest, Ryan," the pastor replied, "I don't think that's a fair classification. Based on this statistic, it's more like playing the odds than playing favorites. The odds are that, if you can get 10% to go 100% in, then the entire group will be impacted."

"Yeah," Pete affirmed, "something happens when the positive passion for God is not just coming from the microphone and message of the youth leader, but from the student next to you. It's almost like the youth pastor's impact is multiplied in powerful ways as a result of him investing his time and life into this core group. He trains them and they in turn reach out to the other students. And the rest of us adult leaders in the group are doing the same thing! In fact, JC actually put me in charge as a co-leader for the core group, so we kind of double whammy leadership for the group.

"Well," Scott interrupted, "good kids are being overlooked by JC and getting their feelings hurt."

"Like your son?" asked Sam pointedly.

"Yeah, like my son!" yelled Scott in a flash of emotion. "I'll be honest with you, Pastor, my son was a key player under Ryan and loved it. But as soon as JC took the position, Chase was forced out."

Ryan stayed quiet. He'd realized early on that choosing Chase to be a part of his student leadership team had been a mistake from square one. Behind his outer, church-faced façade, Chase was a prideful, lust-filled troublemaker. The problem was that, once picked to lead, Ryan hadn't wanted to face the wrath of an angry elder—like JC was facing now in Scott West.

"I wouldn't quite say he was forced out," Pete said. "I was there when JC took him aside and told him that he wanted to talk to him on a deeper level about some areas and attitudes in Chase's life that JC knew your son needed help with. But instead of manning up and having the conversation JC was asking for, Chase chose to drop out of the leadership team.

"That's not what Chase told me," Scott shot back.

"Exactly," Pete said, "he just dropped out because he didn't want to talk to you or JC about it. Instead, he just told you he got 'pushed out,' didn't he?"

"He did," Scott retorted, not even attempting to conceal his anger.

12

CHASE

I hate JC.

Seriously, how dare he push me out of leadership at Spring Valley because he claims to have some insider view into my soul and my motives? Am I perfect? Well, no. But I'm a whole lot better than the group of scrubs he's chosen as his teacher's pets. Maggie? Shane? Josh? Seriously?

My dad has always pushed me to be the best, to be at "the center of influence" no matter what I do. I'm all that at school (Student Body Prez), on our football team (defensive captain) and used to be that in youth group.

But there was no way I was going to talk to JC about that stuff. He asked questions that were way too personal. Like he pulled me aside one night and got in my face about me showing some of the guys some porn photos on my smart phone. I mean, it was before youth group had even started. I'm not even actually sure how he knew what we were even looking at. But it sure sounded like he knew what was going on, so I decided to cut my losses and shut up at that point, 'cuz

I didn't want him going to my dad about it. JC takes all this 'holiness' crap way too seriously. I mean, we're high school guys. What does he expect? And besides, it's not like I'm some drug addict or cutter (like Maggie) or thug (think Shane) or whatever.

Dad would be ticked if he found out that I didn't technically get forced out. But it was the next worst thing. That talk with JC and Pete in the hallway after youth group made me mad.

I guess I took some comfort in the thought that I could sway things my way some with a 'candid' father/son conversations about JC and his leadership style. I'm pretty confident that I can probably get him fired. I'll use my "center of influence" at home to position myself as the victim and JC as the incompetent.

I'll cry to Dad. He'll lean on Ryan and Ryan, my old and reliable youth pastor, will find a way. That dude is smart. Between Dad and him, JC is as good as gone.

Can't wait.

What a jerk.

13

THE LAST STRAW

At dawn he appeared again in the temple courts, where all the people gathered around him, and he sat down to teach them. The teachers of the law and the Pharisees brought in a woman caught in adultery. They made her stand before the group and said to Jesus, "Teacher, this woman was caught in the act of adultery. In the Law Moses commanded us to stone such women. Now what do you say?" They were using this question as a trap, in order to have a basis for accusing him. But Jesus bent down and started to write on the ground with his finger. When they kept on questioning him, he straightened up and said to them, "Let any one of you who is without sin be the first to throw a stone at her." Again he stooped down and wrote on the ground. At this, those who heard began to go away

one at a time, the older ones first, until only Jesus was left, with the woman still standing there. Jesus straightened up and asked her, "Woman, where are they? Has no one condemned you?" "No one, sir," she said. "Then neither do I condemn you," Jesus declared. "Go now and leave your life of sin."

John 8:2-11

"Well, that's everything on the list," Pastor Griffith said, closing up his iPad. "I think most of us can all agree that there's nothing substantial enough to merit a firing. I'll talk to JC tomorrow and we'll tighten some of his methodology up and give him a lesson in tact. But, for the most part, I think we're done here and it's getting late. Meeting adjourned?"

"We're not done, Pastor Griffith," interrupted Scott. "We've saved the best, er, I mean, the worst for last."

With a sigh of frustration Pastor Griffith settled back in his uncomfortable chair and eyed Scott skeptically, "Okay, let's get it over with."

Ryan looked at the pastor and said, "This one is significant."

This grabbed everyone's attention. Pastor Griffith was the first to respond. "Okay, what is it?"

Scott and Ryan looked at each other a few seconds before Scott mumbled, "You tell them."

Everything in the room was quiet, even Agnes stopped her typing and leaned in. Like an actor extending a pause for dramatic effect, Ryan waited a few more seconds before launching into his story.

"Last night A-West's LGBT club shared their views with our kids right here in the youth room. They were invited in by JC himself and treated like royalty while they were here."

Silence.

Agnes couldn't help herself and blurted out the question that hung in the air, "What does LGBT stand for?"

"Lesbian, gay, bi-sexual and transgender," said Scott firmly.

"Why in the world would JC invite them into our youth group?" asked Sam incredulously.

"To interview them and to apologize to them," said Ryan.

"Is he pro-gay or something?" asked Sam. There was anger in his voice and some of the blood drained from his face.

"I think you guys need some context," Pete said, "I was there and it was beautiful."

"Are you pro-gay or something?" asked Sam, turning his angry gaze on Pete.

"Careful, Sam," Pete said while slowly leaning toward him with his biceps flexed and his jaw set.

"I'm serious, guys. I'm with Scott and Ryan on this one. To me, this is a fireable offense," exclaimed Sam.

"I agree," Jim chimed in.

Even Agnes nodded her head "yes" in an acknowledgment that this could be the last straw for JC. With a heavy sigh Pastor Griffith buried his head in his hands, shaking it from side to side.

Filled with renewed confidence that his plan had worked, Scott grabbed Sam's Bible and flipped it open to Romans 1:26-27, ready to put the final nail in JC's coffin. "We all know what the Scriptures say," he said firmly,

> *Because of this, God gave them over to shameful lusts. Even their women exchanged natural relations for unnatural ones. In the same way the men also abandoned natural relations with women and were inflamed with lust for one another. Men committed indecent acts with other men, and received in themselves the due penalty for their perversion.*

Closing the borrowed Bible, Scott sounded like a pastor at the end of a sermon, "Thus saith the Lord."

"Amen!" Jim said, as usual, falling in step with Scott's assessment.

"Pastor?" Agnes asked, gently nudging Pastor Griffith, whose hands still covered his face. "What do you think about all this?"

"I think it's sad," Pastor Griffith said, looking up. "But I would like to know why JC would invite this group into our church. Pete, why would he do something like that?"

"Well, as Ryan already said, for an interview and an apology," Pete said hesitantly, realizing it didn't sound like quite the right thing to say, but at a loss for words that would better capture what had actually happened last night in the youth room.

"We don't understand what you're talking about, Pete, and JC's job is hanging by a thread at this point, so please do some explaining," Pastor Griffith urged.

"Well, you may or may not know that once a month we do a God and Pizza[3] night where we tackle different subjects and everyone invites their friends in, not to get preached at, but to have a discussion," Pete explained, hoping he was choosing the right words to explain the incident in question.

"Right," said the pastor.

"Well, last night's God and Pizza subject was homosexuality and bullying, so JC thought it would be good to have the LGBT club in as our guests. They agreed to attend and to be interviewed," Pete said.

"But they didn't just attend. I learned this morning at church from reliable sources that some of them came in wearing some pretty outrageous outfits. One guy even came in a dress," Ryan said.

"Why didn't you talk to me about it this morning, Ryan?" asked the pastor with a raised eyebrow.

"Well, Pastor, I didn't want to bother you with this before you preached. After I heard about it, I was expecting all sorts of outraged parents would be seeking me out after church, but surprisingly, that didn't happen. I'm not quite sure why. Maybe none of our students even talked about the incident with their parents. Maybe they're so used to the 'diversity' messaging they get at school that they didn't think this was anything out of the ordinary. I don't know. But if I were a parent, I'd be up in arms."

"Well, I am a parent, and I am up in arms," Scott interjected, "though my son wasn't there.

"Still," Pastor Griffith said heatedly, turning back to Ryan, "you should have told me about this after the service this morning."

"Well, er, well," Ryan fumbled, before gathering his excuse and taking the offense. "You left pretty quickly after the last service, so I decided I'd just talk to Scott and ask him for his advice."

"And I," Scott inserted, "talked to Jim and Chris about it right after church and we four elders decided this is an issue that couldn't wait. That's why I called this emergency meeting for tonight."

"Which Chris couldn't make?" Pastor Griffith asked in a frustrated voice.

"He had tickets for the basketball game tonight," Scott said unapologetically. "I told him this was such a clear cut issue, that he really didn't need to be here for the discussion. I was confident the rest of us could handle it."

Pastor Griffith stared at Scott and shook his head in disbelief before turning back to Pete. "So what happened next?" he asked.

"Well, JC asked everyone's opinion on homosexuality and, to be honest, most of the kids even in our youth group said they considered it a lifestyle choice, not a sin."

"And did JC condone it?" asked Pastor Griffith.

"No, as a matter of fact, after about thirty minutes of everyone sharing their opinion, JC read that same passage of Scripture that Scott read earlier and then asked why they thought the Bible was so adamant about God's blueprint for sexuality?"

"I bet they got ticked off then," said Agnes.

"Not really. Maybe it was because JC had really listened to their views. He never affirmed their stance on homosexuality, but he did applaud their honesty," Pete explained. "I think the fact that they felt heard had built a bit of a bridge for some real conversation about the ideas, instead of the usual reactionary name-calling that these kinds of interactions typically illicit."

"What did they think about this passage?" asked Agnes.

"They were all over the board, really. Some thought it was a mistranslation. Others thought that the sin in this passage was promiscuous sex, not homosexual sex. Others thought that maybe there was a deeper reason," said Pete. "Tapping into that deeper reason, JC started with Genesis and shared God's original design for humanity with the story of Adam and Eve. Then he explained how sin entered the picture and screwed everything up. He shared that, from the perspective of the Bible, every sin erupted out of that first sin that perverted God's original design. But, he shared this with such compassion that the teenagers, including those in the gay club, actually listened. And He shared what God did through the cross to rectify the wrong and redeem those who had been lost."

"What happened next?" asked Jim.

"He told them that they didn't have to stop being gay in order to become a Christian," Pete said.

"What! That's blasphemy!" yelled Scott.

"Why? Why is that blasphemy?" Pete yelled back even louder.

"You can't be gay and a Christian at the same time!" Scott bellowed.

"Let me finish what JC said to the group, Scott," Pete shot back, ratcheting the volume down a few degrees. "He told them that they didn't need to get cleaned up before they took a bath, that if they recognized themselves as sinners in need of God's grace and believed the gospel, that the Holy Spirit would come into their lives and begin to transform them from the inside out, just like He did and was doing for every Christian teen in the group. For some it may be immediate, for others it could take a longer time, but he assured them that the good work that God began in them He would complete."

"That's not an unreasonable way to look at it, actually," Pastor Griffith affirmed. "We're all on a journey of transformation. I mean, I still haven't totally conquered lust yet. Have you, Scott?"

"Um, well, I—I—I...," Scott stuttered.

Pete saved him from further embarrassment by commandeering the conversation back to the God and Pizza night. "But what was really beautiful about last night was the apology."

"What apology?" asked Sam, girding himself for more unsettling details.

"Shane's," said Pete.

"The big kid in the leather jacket?" asked Agnes.

"That's the one," Pete said, nodding. "He had been bullying a lot of the—in his words—'sissies' in that group and ever since he became a Christian, he was convicted that he'd been wrong. He stood up and gave the most heartfelt apology I've ever heard. Literally, tears were streaming down his face. The LGBT group stormed the microphone and they all hugged him at the end. There wasn't a dry eye in the place. It was awesome."

"And guess what?" Ryan said. His face looked like a light bulb had just switched on. "Two of them were in church this morning sitting with, of all people, Shane."

"Second service, right?" asked Pastor Griffith.

"Yes," said Ryan, "now that Pete's explained some of the back story, I have better context for the LGBT incident. I guess maybe JC's unconventional approach on this, might actually be—"

"I saw them and remember thinking 'those two don't look like they belong here,' " Pastor Griffith interrupted.

"Shame on you, Pastor," Agnes rebuked softly.

"Yes, shame on me," Pastor Griffith agreed. Turning to Scott, he continued, "Shame on all of us, Scott. This meeting is a sham and it's not going to work."

Scott slammed his fist down on the table and yelled, "Don't you dare lecture me on what's going to work and what is not. JC has deceived Pete, you and, now it looks like, even Ryan! But it doesn't matter, JC is being fired tonight."

"Really? Because you don't have the votes in the room, even if Sam decides to vote your way, we'll be deadlocked fifty-fifty," Pastor Griffith responded tersely.

Scott scowled momentarily. Then his smirk spread across his face. "Well, let's get it on the record, shall we? Who here votes to fire JC?"

Scott and Jim extended their hands upward and looked pointedly at Ryan and Sam. Ryan remained motionless, but tentatively, almost apologetically, Sam raised his hand. "I can't help it," he said, finally turning to look Pastor Griffith in the eye. "I'm just not comfortable with what JC did last night, bringing those homosexuals in here and exposing our students to that kind of lifestyle. So in good conscience I want to go on record against that. It won't make any real difference anyway, since the vote is tied. Maybe, I'm old school, but I can't help it."

"Good for you, Sam!" Scott said, almost crowing. He reached into his pocket and pulled out a piece of paper. "Do you know what this is, Pastor? This is a proxy. Chris gave me his vote by proxy before he left for the game this afternoon. So we have a decision. It's four to three and I win."

Stunned by the proxy maneuver, Pastor Griffith sat in silence.

"Put this in the notes, Agnes," Scott gloated, "according to Article 14 Section 10 of the church bylaws, any staff member can be fired for cause by a majority of voting elders. Based on our four-to-three vote tonight, JC is terminated effective immediately. Furthermore, according to the bylaws no fired staff member can be hired back for a period of at least five years."

Looking over at the pastor, Agnes asked, "Pastor?"

"Looks like West's right," Pastor Griffith admitted with a whisper. "Meeting adjourned."

Pete stormed out of the room in a rage. Scott and Jim left smiling. Everyone else slowly got up and left. Everyone but Ryan.

He sat there and cried. He felt like a Judas.

14

SARAH

I feel like I was born going to church. My family's been here every Sunday and Wednesday since the beginning of time, or at least my time. I'm not whining, I've made a lot of good friends at church over the years. And I've been everything from the baby in the manger to a sheep to Mary in the Christmas play. Under Ryan, youth group became way better than little kid Sunday school. Laser tag nights and lock-ins were a lot of fun and more and more people started coming. I was proud of our big group.

But then JC was put in charge, and he got serious quick. He talked about there being only one way to God, but that wasn't anything new—I'd been hearing that my entire life. Then JC asked us why we were here at youth group and said that he really wanted us to be honest. Some teens said it was because it was fun or because their friends were here. I raised my hand and said, "Because I've always gone to church." JC nodded and said that those were good reasons to go to church, but that there were better reasons: building deep relationships with other Christians, learning about God and about how to apply God's Word to our everyday lives. But the best reason, the real thing that church should teach us, is to own our faith by loving God and loving others.

JC said that our big group was not living up to that potential and that while the teaching and programs would change some, it was us—the students—that really had to change. Our group would only be "dynamic" if each of us loved God all the time, not just in church, and loved people with God's love outside of church. He told us there were just two things he wanted us to really think about that night.

First, JC challenged us about our own faith. He asked why we had faith, what it meant and what we would be willing to sacrifice for it. He told us that faith was meant to be exercised not just talked about...and the best way to exercise our faith was sacrificing something, everything.

That hit home for me.

Church was always just another thing my family did. God and passion might show up in the same song but they weren't two words that went together in my life. JC was giving me a chance here to either admit that God really didn't mean anything to me, or that I did want Him to be really important in my life.

I decided that night that I didn't want to just "go to church" anymore. JC's challenge pushed me to live for something more than myself. To live for a purpose. To live for God.

Secondly, JC challenged us to participate in THE Cause. He explained how while there are many good and worthy causes in our world today, the ultimate cause—THE Cause—is to make disciples who make disciples. And that it's important we be intentional about sharing the Good News of Jesus' grace and forgiveness with those around us in both word and deed. He said we'd be learning all sorts of useful things in youth group about how to actually do this in real life. Like how to start up a natural conversation about God and how to explain the gospel. Stuff like that.

At the end he said that if we were only interested in the "good things": the fun, friends and normalcy of going to church, that we'd be better off finding a different youth group.

I wasn't so sure about THE Cause. I'd just decided that God was important to me. Not just a ritual. But who was I to start pushing my faith at my friends? I went up to talk to JC afterward, to see whether it was okay not to join THE Cause. He listened carefully as I tried to explain why I didn't want to. He was silent and I asked him what he thought about what I said. He asked if we could pray together about it right then to seek God's wisdom. I said sure. He asked if we could both pray, but I told him I'd rather he just pray. So he did.

I was surprised because pastors usually use prayer to just say what they think, or to drive home a sermon. Instead, he thanked God for me and my decision to make God the center of my life. Then he asked God to continue to provide me, him and the rest of the church direction in how we could best love and serve God and people in both word and deed. And that was it. Amen.

JC said that in the weeks ahead, he would be teaching and modeling for us lots of practical "how to's" when it comes to sharing our faith, so it would get less intimidating as we saw how to actually do it.

He said he would keep after me and the whole group about his two challenges. And that we should all keep praying about them.

After that night, a lot of my friends said the group didn't sound like it was going to be fun anymore and they stopped coming. It was really tough.

But during the next several weeks, JC started coming to lunch with me and some of my friends at school. We laugh because he looks too old to be a student, but too happy to be a teacher.

Things changed again for me after Maggie started coming to church. Here was someone who'd never been to church before who was so excited to share about God with everyone she knew. I'd figured out before that I'd just known *about* God instead of knowing Him. But now I understand that the change in my life that comes through knowing God needs to be all encompassing, not just for who I am, but in how I interact with my friends. If knowing God brings me joy, then why shouldn't I want to share that joy with my friends so they can get in on it, too?

I know it took me a couple months, but it's not something I could just be told about. I had to see it. A month ago, I told JC I was ready to sign on for THE Cause. He grinned and asked me what had changed. I said something horribly corny and teenage-girly like "my heart." But that wasn't false.

Now, I'm praying for four of my friends from school and I've started talking to two of them about God. One of them,

Hannah, heard that the LGBT group was coming to church and told me she would be interested in how that turned out, expecting a bloodbath. I told her to come find out for herself, and there'd be free pizza to go with the show. She came! We talked about it afterwards and Hannah said that she'd be back. I'll keep praying, keep asking her questions and keep talking about God.

Things have really changed for me since JC became the youth pastor. Church used to be a ritual for me, but now that God's become something I'm really passionate about, everything's changed. Without JC's challenges I wouldn't have seen past the fun to what God really wants from me and the purpose that He has for my life. JC is all about relationships and his love for people really meshes with what I'm like. I'm still learning what it means to speak the truth in love. But it's really cool because I'm learning that not just from JC, but from other people in youth group, too, and from reading the Bible on my own. (As I seek to share my faith with others, I'm learning a lot more about it, myself!) I seem to err more on the side of love rather than truth, but whether I succeed or fail with Hannah and the rest of my friends, I know that God is making me more courageous and more like Him. I love the fact that my relationship with God is mine and that with Him, nothing is impossible. That's how I hope my friends will feel about God someday, too.

15

RYAN

To be honest, it's actually hard for me to believe that I still have a job. After all, I was a pretty bad egg when it comes to all that plotting and scheming I did with Scott, conspiring for JC's demise.

But my world's flipped upside down and inside out over these past ten days since that fateful meeting where JC was fired. Something changed in me that night. It was like the scales fell off my eyes and I finally got what JC was doing—modeling how to help the hurting and gather the lost, all the while discipling teens to put God at the center of their lives, so they, too, could make disciples who make disciples.

On that somber, stormy Monday morning following the botched elder decision, JC was called into the pastor's office and fired. On his way out, Agnes held onto him with her bony little arms and practically wouldn't let him go. There's nothing quite as heartbreaking as hearing a little old lady cry her eyes out.

But without an ounce of anger or bitterness, he walked out the door, glancing back over his shoulder briefly to call out an encouraging, "Carry on."

Word spread fast that JC'd been fired and a lot of the kids in the youth group were pretty upset about it all. It quickly became clear that JC had a much more devoted following among the teens than his critics ever suspected. That next Wednesday night, the youth room was packed out. And there was plenty of drama, along with buckets of tears. Teens don't just roll over for these kinds of things.

I'd realized in the painful aftermath of that bungled elder meeting that I had to be the one who stood up in front of the youth group to explain everything. I was honest with them. It was painful. I admitted that down deep inside, I'd been intimidated by JC's style of youth ministry and I 'fessed up about the part I'd played in conspiring to push him out. I asked for their forgiveness. Some gave it readily, I think because they saw how genuinely ripped up I was about how things had turned out. But others weren't there yet—anger and betrayal aren't easy emotions to get past. Frankly, I was having a hard time forgiving myself, so how could I blame them?

To honor JC, we turned the end of that meeting into a prayer time. Students prayed that he would have impact in other's lives wherever he went next, just like he'd had in theirs. Then they prayed for the youth group. They prayed for their city and their schools. They prayed to reach every teenager in their Cause Turf with the message of the gospel. And, of course, they prayed for justice to be done in this situation. That the wrong would be made right.

At the next elders meeting it was, in a way.

After JC's firing, Pastor Griffith had done a serious reading of the church's bylaws, looking for a way back from the terrible events that had already been set in motion. In it he discovered that elders were only supposed to serve two two-year terms, after which they were required to step down off the board for a minimum of a year. Because Scott West had been an elder for six years straight with no break, he had to be removed.

That news did not go down well with Scott. He stormed out the door mid-meeting and hasn't been seen at Spring Valley since. I'm pretty sure he's gone for good.

As for me, well, I've made my apologies all around—not just to the teens like I mentioned earlier, but also to Pastor Griffith, to Agnes and the rest of the staff and to the board. And most importantly, to God. My heart breaks with gratitude that we have such a loving and forgiving God. A God of second chances...and third, and fourth, and hundredth and thousandth...

So my world really is flipped upside down and inside out—and that's a very, very good thing. I have a renewed sense of why I got into ministry to begin with. I saw an ugliness inside myself as a result of this whole thing with JC that was painful to look at. But with God's help, I forced myself to. Looking back, I get it now. What had started out as irritation with JC, had morphed into intimidation and finally to a political power play so I could flex my executive pastor muscles.

I was supposed to be his supervisor and it had irritated me to no end that in all our conversations about his unorthodox approach to youth ministry, he always seemed to carry this quiet inner confidence that he knew exactly what he was doing. And here he was, just a former carpenter, while I was the one who had gone to seminary and was the executive pastor. Once people started leaving the church because of him, I'd just had this overriding sense that he was making me look bad and I was determined to take back some control.

Anyway, in the aftermath of it all, I took an honest look at my people-pleasing propensities, my petty positioning and my power play maneuvering and I didn't like what I saw at all. So with God's help, I'm stripping all that away. Only conviction is left, conviction that I need to reinvent my way of ministry. Or, actually, maybe I just need to rediscover it and recapture the same brand of ministry I'd dreamed of in seminary.

On the personal front, Pastor Griffith and I have decided to meet weekly, not for staff stuff, but for heart stuff.

As for Pastor Griffith, moving on is now off the grid for him. In his words, "The grass is greener where you water it." And he's decided to turn on the sprinklers at Spring Valley. No church plant, no executive director position at a nonprofit, no moving away. He's determined to be the pastor at Spring Valley until God moves him from his post. He's excited to see what God can do through him with all (or at least most) of the politics stripped out of the church leadership. And I for one am delighted at his decisions. I think now that we're committed to working together for the same cause—THE Cause—the sky's the limit for Spring Valley's impact on this community.

I got an actual, real life glimpse of this tonight at youth group—the second Wednesday night meeting we've had since

JC was fired. I stood in the back as Maggie led worship, her tears still streaming. I think everyone was expecting me to take the microphone after the opening song, to temporarily fill in the gaping hole that JC left until a new youth leader could be hired. But instead of me taking the microphone, Pete, the big fireman, did.

In the middle of his announcements, he busted out a spontaneous prayer to God with his hands held high and his eyes wide open. He begged God for revival and that the same spirit that fueled JC would fill everyone in the room.

His prayer was answered.

Standing up in the middle of the room right after Pete's "Amen" was Shane, boldly announcing that God had put it on his heart to tell everyone something.

He just stood there for a moment. He didn't look nervous. He just looked really serious. Then he plunged in and told us that we needed to realize that JC is gone and that, for whatever reason, God has moved him on to his new assignment. He acknowledged that we were all going to miss him, but said that he believed that his spirit was right there with us and that, through God's strength, we could complete the mission that he started.

Agnes, who'd signed on to be a youth ministry volunteer just like JC had urged her to, yelled an "Amen" from the back and everyone started clapping.

At that point Sarah suggested we all break up into groups based on our schools and pray for them and ask God to give us wisdom on how to reach our schools with the gospel. Even the homeschooled kids formed their own group to pray for their neighborhoods, sports teams and such. For the rest of the meeting, teens gathered in clusters, interceded on behalf of their schools and classmates and then began to brainstorm how to reach their campuses with the gospel.

Shane and Maggie led the group for A-West. After praying, they talked about starting an open discussion group on campus, kind of like "God and Pizza," where Christian teens would host open dialogues about various topics.

Brandon and Sarah led the group for Spring Valley High. They spent time brainstorming ideas like sitting at different cafeteria tables one day a week so that they could build new relationships with the hope of sharing the Good News. They also talked about creating a prayer ministry at school where they would ask other teenagers what their prayer requests were and then meet regularly to pray for them. In the process, they hoped to create spontaneous and natural spiritual conversations.

It really was amazing. All around the room teens prayed and brainstormed and prayed some more. Some teens got excited enough that they texted their friends right then and there and began the spiritual conversation. It was like it just overflowed. They couldn't keep their mouths shut about God. It actually reminded me of the book of Acts and what God envisioned for the church: prayer, action and revival!

Sure it's gonna be messy, sure some kids—like Michael—were rolling their eyes at all of this stuff, but there is something real going on.

I was the last one to leave the youth room tonight. I'd stayed behind to pray to God that Pastor Griffith and I could spark this same level of transformation in the adults at Spring Valley.

Through the power of Jesus Christ, I know we can.

NOTE FROM THE AUTHOR: WAS JESUS A YOUTH LEADER?

I'll never forget it. I was training a group of pastors at The Billy Graham School of Evangelism about youth ministry. I was talking about the importance of mobilizing the next generation with the Good News of Jesus when an older preacher raised his hand. When I pointed to him, he said something that shocked me.

"Well young man," he stated flatly, "Jesus was a youth leader."

In my mind, I was thinking that he was extrapolating at best and exaggerating at worst. Sure, I wish it were true, but as far as I could tell, there was no Biblical evidence that Jesus was a youth leader.

Trying not to sound condescending, I asked the pastor, "And why do you believe that?"

"Because the Bible says so," was his direct response.

The whole room was riveted as the man of God opened his well worn Bible to Matthew 17:24-27 and read it loudly to all of us,

> *After Jesus and his disciples arrived in Capernaum, the collectors of the two-drachma temple tax came to Peter and asked, "Doesn't*

> *your teacher pay the temple tax?" "Yes, he does," he replied. When Peter came into the house, Jesus was the first to speak. "What do you think, Simon?" he asked. "From whom do the kings of the earth collect duty and taxes—from their own children or from others?" "From others," Peter answered. "Then the children are exempt," Jesus said to him. "But so that we may not cause offense, go to the lake and throw out your line. Take the first fish you catch; open its mouth and you will find a four-drachma coin. Take it and give it to them for my tax and yours"* (Matthew 17:24-27).

The pastor shut his Bible and looked at me as if to say, "I told you so." Not quite understanding how this passage made his point, I asked him to explain.

"Young man, all the disciples went with Jesus into Capernaum, right?" he asked.

"Yes, sir," I responded politely.

"But only Peter and Jesus paid the temple tax," he stated.

"Yes," I answered, still not understanding his point.

He was about to make that point crystal clear by surprising me with his punch line, "According to Exodus 30:14, the temple tax, which was originally that tabernacle tax, was only applicable to those 20 years old and older."

Flipping my Bible open to the Old Testament to double check his reference, it became obvious to me that he was right,

"All who cross over, those twenty years old or more, are to give an offering to the LORD."

The temple tax was only for those twenty years or older. All the disciples were in Capernaum but only Jesus and Peter paid the tax.

If my pastor friend and I are reading these passages right, then Jesus was a youth leader (with only one adult sponsor—Peter!) He had a small budget and a rebellious teen (aka Judas), but with that small youth group he turned the world upside down.

And, if you're a youth leader, you can do the same. The same Holy Spirit that propelled the Son of God empowers you and your teenagers. As you depend on Him, He will do amazing things through your youth ministry efforts.

May this book help you wrestle through the question of, not only what would happen if Jesus was a youth leader, but how you, through the Spirit of Jesus, can implement a more Biblical model of ministry.

God has exciting things in store for you as you keep your eyes on Jesus and unleash your teenagers to follow His example.

And, hopefully, you won't get fired in the process.

END NOTES

[1]Beliefnet.com, "Inspirational Quotes," http://www.beliefnet.com/Quotes/Evangelical/E/E-M-Bounds/What-The-Church-Needs-To-Day-Is-Not-More-Machinery.aspx.

[2]RPI News, *Minority Rules: Scientists Discover Tipping Point for the Spread of Ideas*, http://news.rpi.edu/update.do?artcenterkey=2902.

[3]Shulenburg, Brian, *What's the Deal With...? 500 Questions Today's Students are Asking About the Biggest Issues in Life* (Grand Rapids, MI: Zondervan, 2007), page 7.

ABOUT THE AUTHOR

Greg Stier has been used by God to impact the lives of hundreds of thousands of teenagers across America. He combines amazing true-life stories with his own unique brand of humor to communicate Biblical truth in a way that not only inspires, but equips teenagers for action.

As founder and president of Dare 2 Share, Greg leads his team toward the single goal of mobilizing teenagers to reach their world with the good news of Jesus Christ (Acts 1:8). He is the author of ten books and numerous resources, including *Dare 2 Share: A Field Guide for Sharing Your Faith* and *Ministry Mutiny: A Youth Leader Fable.*

DARE 2 SHARE

Dare 2 Share believes in the power of the gospel and the potential of teenagers.

That's why, at Dare 2 Share, everything we do has one laser focus: to help you energize your students to evangelize their world.

So no matter what you need, we are your source for teen evangelism training and resources.

- Weekend conferences
- Week-long leadership training
- Online training
- Books & curriculum
- Free articles, e-resources, videos & more

Call us at 1-866-448-0272 or visit **www.dare2share.org** to learn more.